Editorial Director: Jonathan Leeman
Managing Editor: Taylor Hartley
Editors: Alex Duke and David Daniels
Copy Editor: Judith Henderson
Executive Director: Ryan Townsend
President: Mark Dever
Cover Design: Odd Notion
Layout Design: Rubner Durais
Paperback ISBN: 979-8-89218-000-9

Tools like this are provided by the generous investment of donors.
Each gift to 9Marks helps equip church leaders with a biblical vision and practical resources for displaying God's glory to the nations through healthy churches.

Donate at: www.9marks.org/donate.
Or make checks payable to "9Marks" and mail to:
    9 Marks
    525 A St. NE
    Washington, DC 20002

info@9marks.org | www.9marks.org

Preparing to Church Plant

Sending Out a Church Plant

Planting a Church

Church Planting in Hindsight

Biblical
Thinking
For

Building
Healthy
Churches

Editor's Note

by Jonathan Leeman

First, a word of thanks to our friends at Pillar Church Planting Network (especially Phil Newton and Matt Rogers) and 20Schemes (especially Matthew Spandler-Davison) for their help on this edition of *Church Matters*. Both ministries have spent more time thinking about church planting than 9Marks has, especially on the practical nuts and bolts of planting. That's why we thought they would be great partners to work with for this edition.

Several themes emerge throughout this volume. Let me mention two. First, church plants and planters are sometimes treated as something other than churches and pastors. They're not. Plants are churches, planters are pastors. Say it twice if it will help you remember.

The reason to emphasize this is the whole world of church planting literature, programs, assessment tools, and workshops over the last few decades too often takes its cues from the business world rather than the Bible. Yet we want your church to think about those would-be planters like

> "Church plants and planters are sometimes treated as something other than churches and pastors. They're not. Plants are churches, planters are pastors."

you would a would-be pastor—according to the qualifications and competencies highlighted by the apostles.

We also want you to think about those plants as churches. Many times, I've heard a planter talk about his one-, two-, or five-year-old "church plant." I'll ask him if they take the Lord's Supper. When he says yes, I suggest he doesn't need to call it a plant anymore. It's a church now, with all the rights, duties, and privileges thereof. My goal in saying that is both to empower

him—"Baby's all grown up!"—but also to subtly remind him that what his church does is constrained by Scripture. The Bible governs churches.

For more on this very theme, see Nathan Knight's excellent new book *Planting By Pastoring.*

A second theme that emerges throughout this volume is the connection between churches and their plants. Biblically ordered and healthy churches tend to plant biblically ordered and healthy churches. Biblically disordered and unhealthy churches tend to plant the same. That's not to say you need to wait till your church is in tip top health before planting. It does mean that what your church aspires to will transfer. After all, kids value what their parents value. That means the first step of planting might be to consider your own church's health.

We at Pillar, 20Schemes, and 9Marks pray you find this edition of *Church Matters* edifying and instructive.

Jonathan edits all 9Marks titles as well as Church Matters. He is the author of several books focusing on ecclesiology. Jonathan earned his MDiv from Southern Seminary and a Ph.D. in Ecclesiology from the University of Wales. He lives with his wife and four daughters in Cheverly, Maryland, where he is an elder at Cheverly Baptist Church.

Section One

Preparing to Church Plant

The Priority of Patience, Prayer, and Preaching in Church Planting

by Josh Manley

I pastor an ordinary church in an extraordinary part of the world. My city, Ras Al Khaimah, is in the United Arab Emirates. It's extraordinary because it's situated near the tip of the Arabian Peninsula, and eleven and a half years ago the ruling Sheikh granted land for an evangelical church building here.

Yet, the church that's been planted here is ordinary. Hopefully, what marks our church is what would mark any faithful church in any part of the world.

So if you've come to this article looking for a new technique or tips on how to develop and strengthen your brand, you'll be disappointed. Because the church is the demonstration of the wisdom of God, we must be careful that our labors to pursue its growth and health don't derive from man's wisdom but God's. God-centered ends are accomplished by God-given means.

> "Because the church is the demonstration of the wisdom of God, we must be careful that our labors to pursue its growth and health don't derive from man's wisdom but God's."

Therefore, church planter, before you do anything else, you must prioritize three things: patience, prayer, and preaching.

PATIENCE

Among the many images we find in Scripture for the work of ministry, one common principle is the necessity of patience in the work of the kingdom. Think of the farmer sowing his seed (Mark 4:14; Jas. 5:7).

From the beginning, Christians have always been marked out as a waiting people, as many of our fathers "died in faith, not having received the things promised, but having seen them and greeted them from afar" (Heb. 11:13). We serve the God who sees the end from the beginning, who gets particular glory by taking what seems small and unimpressive to this world and slowly growing it into something astonishing, that which can only be explained by his power (Zech. 4:10; Matt. 13:31–32). Among other things, the drama of redemptive history will definitively prove that God was incredibly patient both with his creatures and in his great work of salvation.

As we think about church planting, we must refuse to move quickly when our God is pleased to move slowly. While it may not fit with the zeitgeist of our culture and times, we trust deep, lasting change that's rooted in the gospel doesn't happen overnight. Yes, our God grants breakthroughs and revivals. But for those moments to be genuine and lasting, they must come on God's terms and by his ways.

Pastoral patience demands we labor by faith, trusting that our God knows how to spread and protect the gospel better than we do. For example, when a pastor friend of mine began laboring in his new church, the congregation wasn't yet ready to receive the Bible's teaching on elders. Rather than rush the church toward where they "needed" to be, he waited patiently—for ten years! He knew it would be wrong to split the church over this issue, so he led by teaching and praying until the church was ready. Now that church is thriving under their leadership and bearing much fruit.

Church planters, prioritize patience.

PRAYER

Charles Spurgeon famously called the church prayer meeting "the powerhouse of the church." If it's good for the church, then surely it's good for the church planter.

Of all the good endeavors the apostles could have given themselves to in the early church—both "when the disciples were increasing in number" and when there was conflict between the Hellenists and Hebrews over the neglect of widows—what did they do? They devoted themselves "to prayer and to the ministry of the word" (Acts 6:1, 4). Prayer was pivotal to the election of the first deacons (Acts 6:6), evangelism (Acts 4:31), Peter's release from prison (Acts 12:5, 12), strength in the midst of suffering and imprisonment (Acts 16:25), the health of the Ephesian church and her leaders (Acts 20:36), and the overall work of God in the advance of the gospel.

If your vision to plant a church doesn't include a commitment to public and private prayer, then your vision needs correcting. When the new and cutting-edge is valued over the wisdom of the ages, we're subtly submitting ourselves to human cleverness and therefore diminishing our desperate need to pray for the power of God. If our efforts to plant churches aren't attended to by steady, disciplined, private prayer, then what reason do we have to think our churches will reach beyond our generation and into future ones?

The problem with relying too heavily on church planting techniques or brands or methods that make sense in one particular cultural moment is that our cultural moment will soon pass and give way to another. So, if you've planted your church while relying on all the wisdom this current cultural moment can give you, just know it's prone to fade with the passage of time.

Consider instead how it pleases God to expose the wisdom of this world in its folly (1 Cor. 3:19). Unseen by this world, a steady commitment to prayer is seen by our God who is pleased not only to hear but also to act.

Church planters, prioritize prayer.

PREACHING

As the apostle Paul languished in a Roman prison waiting to be executed by the state, he had to consider carefully what advice he should give to Timothy about the future of the church. Of all the advice he could have given, it might surprise us that he narrowed in on preaching: "Preach the Word; be ready in season and out of season" (2 Tim. 4:2). Paul banked the future of the young, emerging, and even fledgling church on the proclamation of the Word of God.

As you think about church planting, will it be evident that you're wholly dependent on the Word to build the church? The true church is built on the Word of God rightly preached. If that's not what's primarily building your church plant, then you may want to ask if you've really planted a church.

From the beginning to the end, the Scriptures make it clear that God gets particular glory when it's obvious his Word is creating and gathering a people. Giving time and attention to preaching makes clear where the church is centered. And as a congregation sits under the preached Word, it makes a statement that in the midst of a world opposed to God, this Word needs to be heard, and we need to humble ourselves before it. We joyfully and carefully submit ourselves to the revealed Word of God in order to know and make known the revealed God of the Word.

So, church planters, prioritize preaching, realizing that as you do you give yourself to the biblically sure means that God himself has promised to bless in time.

CONCLUSION

For the past ten and a half years, I've labored to plant and pastor a biblical church in a part of the world that desperately needs a gospel witness. While it's an extraordinary place to plant a church, the work to plant it has been pretty ordinary. While the church must always be reforming, reform runs amok when the revealed wisdom of Scripture has been marginalized to make room for the latest pragmatic wisdom.

So, church planters, as you patiently "preach and pray, love and stay," you'll find that your church has been planted on fertile soil that bears up good and lasting fruit.

Josh Manley is a Pastor of RAK Evangelical Church in the United Arab Emirates. You can find him on Twitter at @JoshPManley.

Why Not to Plant Churches

by Phil Newton

Since the late 1980s, I've engaged many pastors and would-be pastors regarding church planting. I generally ask why they desire to plant. Sometimes the response lacks sound reason. Let me offer a few reasons *not* to plant churches.

TAP THE BREAKS

1. Don't plant a church to escape from dealing with pastoral issues.

Perhaps a brother faces the long, grinding work of biblical reformation, and so he wonders about planting. The fact is, we might not solve our problems by planting another church. We might just take our problems with us. Dealing with membership issues, honesty in church rolls, or church discipline challenges every pastor. Who can blame a pastor for leaving—unless, of course, one is called by God to shepherd his flock?

Escaping difficulties by planting a church will only ensure that different difficulties will follow. When I planted a church after pastoring three other churches, I thought I would leave behind many of the typical issues faced by SBC pastors. I did leave *some* of them behind, but I inherited other issues common to church starts.

You cannot escape. Issues come with the territory. People come with problems. But that's why God has called you to the work: to point your congregation to Christ and his glory in all things; to serve as an example of godliness in trying times; to feed the flock the Word of God; to nurture and admonish them to follow Christ; to apply the gospel to every area of life.

2. Don't plant a church on impulse.

Impulsiveness implies no strategy or increasing burden by the Spirit, just a mess that looks for a quick solution.

Church splits have mothered many new churches. Trouble brews. A fight erupts. Sides are chosen. *Presto!* A new church is formed.

Mercifully, in God's sovereign kindness, many good churches have started out of splits. These churches have legitimate reasons for their start if they've faithfully pursued reconciliation to no avail. If a split occurs over disagreement on the color of the carpet or the time Sunday School begins, then humility and repentance must prevail over an abrupt departure.

However, if a split occurs over the gospel, the essentials of the faith, qualified church leadership, maintaining regenerate membership, or exercising biblical church discipline, then a new church might be necessary. I say *might* because these doctrinal issues can possibly be worked out with patient, humble teaching.

Never rush to plant in a moment of impulsiveness. Seek to display the spirit of Christ in all things. Only when serious doctrinal and gospel issues cannot be resolved must a split occur for the sake of Christ's glory in the community. And in that setting, the new church must never swagger with pride that they are the *real* church. Trouble could follow the new church, too, so give care to approach starting a new work with humility.

3. Don't plant a church as a problem-solving panacea.

Such idealism exalts man rather than the Lord of the church. Sinners are always messy, including the sinner who happens to be the church planter. New churches bring their own problems.

> "Starting a new church doesn't eliminate problems unless you eliminate people, and that's not the goal of a new church."

I still faced hidden agendas, unorthodox beliefs, personality conflicts, leadership struggles, financial woes, and a bag full of other issues when I planted a church. Starting a new church doesn't eliminate problems unless you eliminate people, and that's not the goal of a new church.

4. Don't plant a church just because it seems the only option to be a pastor.

Some men view church planting as the means to secure a pulpit. This brings up an important matter: when more pastoral candidates exist than open pulpits, it might be a clear indication that some of that waiting number need to plant churches.

But not all of them; some need to be seasoned a bit longer before starting a new church. Churches do not need to be planted to accommodate men but to exalt Christ.

Some men lack the necessary gifts and calling to pastor, but nonetheless think that they must have a church. Others are harsh and inflammatory, having caused divisions by their personality foibles. So they seek to plant a church where everyone will cooperate with them and overlook their unsanctified personality. Beginning a church to suit such a man lacks legitimacy.

CONSIDERING RIGHT MOVES

So what is a good answer to the question of why someone should want to plant a church? Why start from scratch without any history or tradition, without leadership structure or educational organization, without financial backing or arrangements, without a building or suitable location? Why do it? I would boil a good answer down to three right motives.

First, you should see *the need* for a new church, not to escape problems but to establish a biblical ministry to reach people for the sake of God's kingdom. The need is not for a preacher's platform but for Christ's glory among a people.

Second, you should sense *the call* of God on your life to do this work. Test it and weigh it. Evaluate your motives, and consider the demands involved. If none of this deters you from planting a church, then move to the next preliminary steps.

Third, you should hear *the affirmation* of the spiritually mature in your present church. Test your sense of calling with your pastors, wife, and spiritual mentors. Are they in agreement? Do they recognize God's preparation in your life and the unique abilities entrusted to you for such a work? The last step: are you willing to risk all for the sake of establishing a new church to the glory of Christ? Only then are you ready to consider planting a church.

YES, PLANT

You might get the idea that I want to talk brothers out of church planting. That's not the case, but I'm concerned that my brothers understand the demand of Christ as they ponder starting a new church.

They will wear unexpected hats. They must be willing to work long and hard hours, often working another job to meet family needs. They must be willing to trust others who will join them, sharing the load, distributing responsibilities, training leaders, investing in people, and cultivating teachers. They must be accountable to others spiritually, financially, morally, ethically, and ecclesiologically. They must get in the lives of the people among whom they are seeking to establish a church, sharing their joys and sorrows, knowing their heartaches and trials.

Planters must be teachable, realizing there will be plenty of "firsts" that cross the threshold. They will make mistakes and must humbly admit them. They will need course corrections from time to time as their "best-laid plans" fizzle. In God's providence, this re-directs the new church's ministry. They must be

> "Yes, plant churches. But do so after counting the cost."

flexible in plans and organization but unbending in doctrine and commitment to gospel ministry.

Yes, plant churches. But do so after counting the cost. And then joyfully plunge forward.

Phil A. Newton is director of pastoral care & mentoring for the Pillar Network after serving 44 years as a senior pastor.

Preparing to Plant Is a Whole Church Effort

by Dwayne Milioni

Yesterday morning I received a text message from my assistant who is planting a church in a Korean neighborhood of Queens, NY. It read, "Please pray that I will find an apartment large enough for my family in the next two days." Finding housing, decent schools, and rental space large enough for a church to gather are just a few challenges church planters face. Last night, my small group prayed for God's favor on his behalf. The journey of church planting should involve the entire congregation.

Equipping and sending teams to plant gospel-centered churches has been a substantial effort of my church since 2005, when our congregation voted to emphasize church multiplication vs. church addition. If the Lord wills, the team we send to Queens will be our 20th plant. How can church planting and revitalization become essential to your church's strategy?

A biblical strategy for missions should begin and end with the local church. For my church, it looks as follows:

1. A commitment by the local church to fulfill its biblical obligation (Acts 1:8)
2. To proclaim the gospel through the power of the Holy Spirit (Acts 6:7)
3. So that people will repent and place saving faith in Jesus Christ (Acts 2:37–41)
4. And be equipped by pastors for the work of ministry (Eph. 4:11–13)
5. To send church members to begin new, autonomous local churches (Acts 13:2–3)
6. And cooperate with other like-minded churches to eventually repeat the process (Acts 14:21–28)

"The journey of church planting should involve the entire congregation."

Through prayer, God has blessed this strategy. What might a "whole church" approach to planting look like for you? It will involve preparing, sending, and ongoing engagement of church planters and their teams.

PREPARING

Getting members to commit to multiplication through church planting is a long process. The goal is for church planting to seep into the roots of a church's DNA. An excellent place to begin is with your church's membership process. My church stresses the importance of missions in our membership class. We inform prospective members they are joining a sending church, and we hope that some of them will eventually be sent out on one of our church plant teams.

Preparation also occurs through preaching and teaching. As the church's mission shows up in Scripture, teachers can make direct applications about church planting. Also, when the church gathers to pray, the congregation can seek the Lord on behalf of their current and future church plants. You can even pray often for God's help.

Getting your church's small groups involved in church planting also helps. The members of your church who enjoy close fellowship with those being sent tend to take more ownership of the church plant. In addition, invested members become good points of contact between the church plant team and the rest of the church.

If your church hopes to send church planters regularly, you might invest in a formal residency or internship program. A residency provides the means to equip and prepare church planters. Some churches choose short, intensive internships (six months to a year). Other residencies are less intensive and longer. These programs allow for in-depth training in biblical ecclesiology and the proper missiology that should extend from it. You can also address pastoral theology and practice. In addition, internships may include personal discipleship. At my church, we pair elders with interns, and they meet regularly for training, counseling, and prayer.

The goal is to create a funnel that continually filters through church members—pulling out impurities, refining their giftedness, and preparing them for future ministry. My church provides a two-year equipping ministry for both men and women. In addition, lead church planters are given a third year of residency. Typically, they will join our church staff to receive more direct ministry experience. Future church planters tend to spend five to ten years at our church. This may seem long, but since we continually pour members through our "funnel," we can send church plant teams regularly.

SENDING

One of the great joys of the local church is sending off teams. Acts describes a "whole church" celebration of sending (Acts 13:3–5). It has become a tradition to lay hands and commission those being sent.

Sending gives church plant teams a strong sense of approval and affirmation that they are doing the Lord's work. It also strengthens the church to witness members go out and do difficult things for the gospel. Sending allows the entire congregation to take ownership of the process. Even though your church may lose key members, sending does not subtract from the church. Instead, it strengthens and motivates the church to remain on mission. It has been amazing to watch God replace those we have sent.

ENGAGING

Another critical responsibility of the whole church is to provide ongoing support for their church planting teams. Parachurch ministries and agencies are often involved with church planters for the first several years. This can be beneficial for both the church plant and the sending church. Eventually, these agencies will discontinue their support. Many church plants fail to thrive after the first three years. They still need help and encouragement from their sending church.

I am often pleased to hear my members engaging with those we have sent out. Ongoing relationship between mother-and-daughter churches benefit both. This involves prayer, communication, and short-term trips for encouragement and support.

Church plants often struggle with a lack of resources and a lack of mature believers to bear the load of ministry. Planters also struggle with loneliness and fear of failure. Just as it takes years to train and watch a child mature, we must patiently come alongside and care for our church plants as they mature.

My church has been blessed to engage with our plants for over a decade. We recently celebrated the ten-year anniversaries of two of our plants, along with the birth of two "granddaughter" church plants.

A COUPLE WARNINGS

The ongoing process of preparing, sending, and engaging takes time and financial resources. Effective church planting demands a commitment from the elders, especially the regular preaching pastor. It is easy to forget those who have been sent. Please do not let "out of sight, out of mind" occur. Keep your church planters before your congregation.

Also, do not neglect the wives and single adults you are sending. Most of the attention and support tends to go to the lead planter. His wife and other team members are making equal commitments to pack up their lives and move. The sending church should make a special effort to encourage and care for the entire team. Those who commit to being bi-vocational church plant members have additional responsibilities. They must hold down jobs on top of their roles at the new church. Consider this, so the whole team remains healthy and useful.

Dwayne Milioni, PhD serves as lead pastor of Open Door Church in Raleigh, NC

You Can't Plant a Church If You Don't Know What a Church Is

by Nathan Knight

So, you're thinking about planting a church.

What do you think you need? The gospel? Yes. The enabling power of the Spirit? Yes. A sending church? Yes. Others to go with you? Yes. Some money? Probably.

But what about a robust ecclesiology?

Ecclesiology can't be assumed, nor should it be considered a distraction to the church planter's "mission." It also can't be a kind of add-on that you insert here and there as you have need. Instead, ecclesiology should inform, instruct, and even excite the mission of planting churches to the glory of God.

In other words, church planter, you need a robust ecclesiology that's in place well before you start trying to plant a church.

A church is more than a gathering of people around preaching and singing. There are brightly defined lines that have been given to us by the Lord. These lines mark Christians off from the world so as to picture a better city in which we'll all live for eternity. We must take the time to think through these lines and carefully institute them for the good of our neighbor and the glory of God.

> "ecclesiology should inform, instruct, and even excite the mission of planting churches to the glory of God."

Several of us planted Restoration Church inside the District of Columbia in 2010. Allow me to walk you through four of the questions that were instructive to us as we began our work.

1. What is a church?

It sounds ridiculously simplistic, but answering this question proved to be one of the most helpful things we did.

Was our Bible study a church? Was the gathering of people with music and preaching a church? How did we know we "succeeded" in planting a *church*?

The "church" (*ekklesia*) in the Bible is a group of believers who regularly gather together for preaching and covenanting together through the ordinances.

This definition requires several things:

- A regular gathering
- The proper preaching of God's Word (Proclaim the Gospel)
- The proper administration of the ordinances (Portray the Gospel)
- Restorative church discipline (Protect the Gospel)

Armed with that definition and those three descriptions, we knew both what our goal and success looked like.

2. Who makes up the church?

The answer to this question might seem easy except for all those warnings in the Bible of false teachers, professors who don't endure, and those who do things in the name of the Lord but are never actually known by him. Therefore, we knew we needed to be careful about who identified with the church.

Texts like Matthew 16:13–20 and 18:15–20 wonderfully instructed us. They helped us see our responsibility to carefully define the gospel message and to declare who possessed that message, which is want it means to "bind and loose."

Because of this, we also spent time teaching on the gospel and what it looked like to live as a Christian. Only after this did we begin to welcome those around us into the membership of the church (1 Cor. 12).

3. Who takes the ordinances?

Once the definition of a church and the members of the church were clarified, we began to discuss the relationship between the church and the ordinances of baptism (Matt. 28:19–20, Rom. 6:1–4) and the Lord's Supper (Mark 14:22–25; 1 Cor. 11:17–33).

The ordinances were given to the church as signs or markers of the ambassadors of the kingdom. Therefore, we knew instinctively not to practice them until we'd become a church.

On March 28, 2010, our would-be church held a ceremony whereby members covenanted together in accordance to our statement of faith and a church covenant. Another man and I were subsequently installed as elders and only after that did we take the Lord's Supper together, thereby "officially" making us a church.

You can imagine the joy of those eighteen people that night as we became a church. The very thing we'd been praying, teaching, and talking about for many months finally became a reality. A church had been planted, and Christ was exalted as yet another gathering of Christians had been marked off from the world through the bright, bold lines of membership, baptism, and the Lord's Supper.

4. What's my job as a pastor?

We were installed as pastors because our people had been instructed on what to look for in the Pastoral Epistles (1 Tim. 3:1–7, Titus 1:5–9). Once we'd become a church and been officially called as pastors, we took our cues from Acts 6:1–6 and 20:17–35.

These passages told us the bulk of our work was to preach, pray, watch out for wolves, shepherd the flock, watch ourselves, care for our families, and make disciples. Hebrews 13:17 stood prominently in our minds as well: we'll answer to God for how we've led these people.

Ecclesiology Matters

A clear ecclesiology on the front end defined our orientation for church planting. It directed us, encouraged us, and kept us focused on God's plan for his people. The work was hard, and it continues to be. But we've never regretted wielding the sword of God's Word in the difficult work of planting churches.

Ecclesiology is one of God's methodologies for glory. It doesn't slow or deviate from mission. Instead, it fuels the church's mission by marking off God's people from the world. Paul wrote to one local church and told them that they were "lights . . . in the midst of a crooked and twisted generation" (Phil. 2:15).

Church planter, think through these questions now. Don't wait to institute clear convictions after you've gathered a crowd, but carefully put them in place as you go. Explain to those around you what you are or are not doing, so they can be informed for the good of their neighbor and the glory of God.

Nathan Knight is the pastor of Restoration Church in Washington, D.C.

Partnering Together to Plant

by Nathan Akin

W hile much of the conversation around cooperation in the New Testament occurs in descriptive language, John's third epistle raises cooperation to the level of imperative: "we *ought* to support people like these, that we may be fellow workers for the truth" (3 John 8, emphasis added).

The conviction that independent churches should work interdependently with one another to plant new churches drove the Association of Irish Baptist Churches to form. In 1895, 27 Irish Baptist churches formalized themselves into an association after siding with Spurgeon and breaking from the Baptist Union amidst the Downgrade Controversy. Now 125 years later, that Association has grown by over 100 churches because of cooperation and sharing resources to establish new works.

Sometimes cooperation can be difficult among brothers. I grew up with three brothers and no sisters. We fought all the time. My poor mom basically lived in a male dormitory filled with WWF wannabes. I cannot help but wonder if my mom's favorite passage was an adaptation of Psalm 133, "How good and sweet it is when the Akin brothers dwell in unity." Now, though, I am incredibly close with my brothers, and we communicate almost every day. They are all involved in gospel ministry. Though our relationship used to be marked by competitiveness, today we do everything we can to make sure one another flourishes.

If that is true for biological brothers, how much more should it be true for those who are "not bound by blood ties alone but are brothers after the Spirit and in God?"[1]

Cooperation is built on a theological foundation. Pastors, we are brothers! This theological truth shows up in basically every New Testament epistle. And part of what the New Testament calls us to is cooperation in the mission that God has given to his church. While churches are independent and autonomous, they also are interdependent for the sake of those who don't know the Lord. This is primarily accomplished through starting and strengthening churches.

> "While churches are independent and autonomous, they also are interdependent for the sake of those who don't know the Lord."

The New Testament highlights at least two reasons for cooperation: 1) we can do *better* together; and 2) we can do *more* together.

1. BETTER TOGETHER

In the New Testament, churches partner together for mutual influence and help.

For example, in Acts 11 a report comes to the church in Jerusalem that a good number of Gentiles in Antioch have been converted, and they send one of their members named Barnabas to help the church in Antioch. When Barnabas arrives, he's encouraged: "When he came and saw the grace of God, he was glad, and he exhorted them all to remain faithful to the Lord with steadfast purpose" (Acts 11:23).

Interestingly, Jerusalem does not send an Apostle but a helper; Jerusalem is not acting as an authority but a partner. Barnabas is glad to see the grace of God displayed through the flourishing of other churches. So he exhorts them to remain faithful with steadfast purpose. This is the sort of sharpening that should happen through our partnerships.

The churches of the New Testament also exercise doctrinal accountability with one another. Consider Acts 15. Some use this chapter to push hierarchical cooperation, but take a step back and observe the pattern of mutual partnership. Jerusalem does not call for the meeting. Antioch takes the initiative by sending Paul and Barnabas to Jerusalem. Luke records,

> Paul and Barnabas and some of the others were appointed to go up to Jerusalem to the apostles and the elders about this question. . . When they came to Jerusalem, they were welcomed by the church and the apostles and the elders,

and they declared all that God had done with them. (Acts 15:2b, 4)

The church at Antioch had been stirred up by troublesome teaching that threatened the gospel. To get greater clarity, they sought out counsel from another church. Through cooperation, both churches are sharpened by the clarifying of doctrine and practice.

The New Testament also records partnering for financial help in places like 1 Corinthians 16 and 2 Corinthians 8–9. Paul commends the churches of Macedonia for giving generously to the church at Jerusalem. Interestingly, these churches help the original church—the first ever church plant. Churches help one another because we are better together.

What might this look like in our day? It might look something like The Pillar Network: partnership and sharpening by welcoming other churches in matters of confessions, covenants, constitutions, philosophy of ministry, help, and finances for the starting and strengthening of churches. For instance, Pillar often helps both plants and revitalizations as they form new covenants, constitutions, staff policies, non-profit status, websites, payroll help, and more. Our goal is to model the collaboration we find in the New Testament.

2. MORE TOGETHER

Paul and others sought to obey the Great Commission through planting and strengthening churches all over the world. We should follow his lead.

We see this in Acts 13–14 as Paul and Barnabas go out to proclaim the Word

(Acts 13:15–49), preach justification by faith (Acts 13:39), establish churches (Acts 14:23), and appoint elders (Acts 14:23). In Acts 16, the church at Lystra releases a faithful member named Timothy who is "well-spoken of by the brothers" (Acts 16:2). They do this so he can join Paul, a man commissioned by Antioch (Acts 13–14), and a partnership forms for starting and strengthening churches.

Likewise, Pillar, like so many other church networks, regularly gets to witness the blessing of cooperation. Recently, a Pillar church in North Carolina sent a young man they had trained to a Pillar church in South Carolina. Similarly, Pillar just helped a planter and the group of churches cooperating to help him establish his church plant. Over the course of six months, that planter preached at a handful of other Pillar churches in the area. The result? All six churches sent people and money to help establish the new work. Those sorts of stories happen again and again as churches send leaders to do everything from lead music to pastor.

This kind of partnering work is also consistent with what we see in the Epistle to the Romans. While this letter is rightly viewed as a theological masterpiece, Paul hammers home that he is writing for the sake of partnering together in the Great Commission. Paul writes in Romans 15:24, "I hope to see you in passing as I go to Spain, and to be helped on my journey there by you. . ." Paul saw partnership together with the Roman church as strategic to ongoing church planting. In fact, some have argued that Romans is one big missionary support letter.

CONCLUSION

It's true that we can do far more together than apart, but we must be intentional in our efforts to partner together. Who knows what the Lord will do? What an immense privilege to serve the King together as brothers and sisters. May this unity for starting and strengthening churches lead to continued gospel fruit, "as indeed in the whole world it is bearing fruit and increasing" (Col. 1:6b).

---

1. *Aristides (*The Apology of Aristides, *translated by Rendel Harris [London: Cambridge, 1893].*

Nate Akin is the Executive Director of the Pillar Network

Pastor, Not Entrepreneur

by Nathan Knight

Imagine being on a first date with someone who spent the whole evening emphasizing a love for Mario Brothers. Imagine being served by a chef who emphasizes how good a store-brand steak sauce is. Or imagine riding with a helicopter pilot who emphasizes how new he is to flying.

Emphasis matters.

When it came to making disciples and planting churches, Jesus or Paul never emphasized being entrepreneurial. It's true, they believe hell is real and that making disciples and planting churches is desperately urgent. Yet this never led them to highlight industriousness or creativity for church planters. Instead, they emphasized character (1 Tim. 3:1–7, Titus 1:5–8), conviction (1 Tim. 4:1–4, Titus 1:9), and capability (1 Tim. 3:2) for church planters. They underlined the need for men who taught the gospel faithfully and embodied that message in their daily lives.

"Jesus or Paul never emphasized being entrepreneurial."

They emphasized character, capability, and conviction because they knew a few things we tend to forget. They knew that the devil prowled and was powerful. They knew that the spirit was willing but the flesh was weak. And they knew the world was enticing.

The first church planters knew, as Jesus taught, that several kinds of soils produce people who profess faith in Christ but bear no fruit. Only one kind of soil produces believers who will endure (Mark 4:1–20). The Lord loses none of his sheep, but the attrition rate for those who profess Christ in the world is high. Therefore, the apostles emphasized planting churches with men who were sturdy, not men with creativity or charisma who planted with straw.

BUSINESS CAPTIVITY OF THE CHURCH

Martin Luther famously wrote a book amidst the early fires of the Reformation entitled *The Babylonian Captivity of the Church*. In it he critiques the corruption of the Roman Catholic Church. I wonder if someone should write a book entitled, "The Business Captivity of the Church." The author could expose contemporary people's trust in their industry to produce kingdom results.

I once participated in a church planting ministry's vetting of potential planters where the thrust of the time was spent evaluating the potential planter's ability to start something from nothing. They had to write out their calling and vision, present it, and defend it. They had a "speed dating" exercise where they were asked questions and evaluated by how they answered. This same organization has also asked planter candidates to present their work to the tune of music from the business reality television show *Shark Tank*.

Emphasis matters.

It's hard to find a church planting book, conference, or website where the word "entrepreneur" doesn't come up quickly. It's not a sinister word or concept in and of itself. It's sometimes helpful. But the frequent use of the word often points to a goal of getting church plants to grow as fast as possible for the sake of financial security and multiplication. These two things become the evaluative lenses by which planters are assessed.

To be sure, we should all want financial security and multiplication, but by emphasizing the fruit of ministry, you run the risk of de-emphasizing the root of ministry: a heart for God and his people.

Emphasizing the acumen of Wall Street and the values of Silicon Valley in what to look for in a planter distracts us from paying attention to the New Testament's emphases—who a man is.

STURDY CHURCH

Think of the story of the three little pigs. The first two quickly build houses of straw and sticks and make fun of the third pig who painstakingly builds with bricks. They make fun, that is, until the wolf blows down their houses and they retreat to the bricks.

We need churches made of bricks. We need planters who are assessed on what Paul emphasizes. We need sturdy churches led by men with spines of steel and hearts of compassion. We need pastors, not entrepreneurs.

LOVE NEVER FAILS

There's one more thing Jesus emphasized that we overlook in evaluating church planters. Not only should our evaluations emphasize character, capability, and conviction; we should also emphasize a planter's love.

At the conclusion of his church planting residency, Jesus asked his lead planter three times if he loved him. As Peter responded positively each time, our Lord answered by telling him to feed and tend his sheep (John 21:15–19).

Love for Christ leads to compassionate care for the sheep he purchased with his own blood. This was Jesus's final evaluation as he commissioned Peter to go out and plant churches, a call that Peter was evidently struck by, as he commanded it to the dispersion later (1 Pet. 5:1–4).

Love is not efficient in the business sense. It's willing to finish last now for the sake of finishing first in the end. Love is slow—it's patient. Love is kind—not pushy. Love does not insist on its own way—it insists on the Lord's way of bearing crosses, not earthly crowns. Love sees the people it's preaching to and praying for. Love doesn't look for crowds built quickly, but a people built intentionally together. This kind of love never fails—ever (1 Cor. 13:1–8).

It is for this reason that Paul counsels his young disciple Timothy that our aim is love which issues from a pure heart, a good conscience, and a sincere faith (1 Tim. 1:5). Our driving passion for moving into a community to start a church is not to get things going as quickly as possible—it's to love. Love for Christ and love for his blood-bought sheep.

Therefore, planter-pastor, aim at love when you set out to start a new assembly for Christ. Love the character of Christ, love the convictions of Christ, and plead for the capability to proclaim Christ in that love. Then love Christ by feeding and tending his sheep. Whatever comes as a result of that will be enough. Because this kind of love never fails.

Nathan Knight is the pastor of Restoration Church in Washington, D.C.

Pastor, Not Entrepreneur, Part 2

by Matt McCullough

W hen I was first assessed as a church planter, people often asked me if I thought of myself as an entrepreneurial type. I believe it was a fair question.

It was fair in part because of my background. Imagine the question asked with eyebrows raised: you think *you're* an entrepreneur? At that point I'd never started anything in my life besides a long sequence of degree programs. My full-time work had been as a small cog in a large university wheel that didn't need me to keep rolling. Like most grad students, I was all too happy to keep reading and writing and teaching in the narrow lane of my chosen field, talking only to the few people who were already interested or the slightly larger crowd who were assigned to pay attention. Whatever a typical church planter may be, I didn't fit the mold.

But that common question made sense, given my background, because of a common assumption that lies just beneath its surface. I believe we often assume church planting requires more entrepreneurial skills than other pastoral contexts. Is that a fair assumption? Should church planters be entrepreneurs?

IT CAN BE HELPFUL

Of course, the answer to that question depends on what we mean by entrepreneur. The Oxford English Dictionary defines an entrepreneur as a "person who sets up a business or businesses, taking on financial risks in the hope of profit." At Harvard Business School, an entrepreneur is one who pursues "an opportunity beyond resources controlled."

These definitions come from a business context that doesn't map exactly onto a local church context, but you can likely see why we associate church planting and entrepreneurship. Church planters set something up from scratch. They do that where they've identified an important opportunity, some sort of gap in what's already available. And they often have to be comfortable making up for limited resources with their own time, sweat, creativity, and flexibility.

As a church planter, you have to be willing to do whatever needs to be done. You can't rely on a well-oiled machine in which you have a limited role to play, doing only what you're good at while other specialists handle everything else. Because there are no systems in place, you have to be able to plan, to see the big picture, and to recognize what steps to take in what order to reach your goals. You've got to deal with constant context-shifting, and you can't be above the range of menial tasks each day might bring.

BUT IT'S NOT NECESSARY AND IT'S NOT SUFFICIENT

All that said, I'm living proof that new churches can thrive without entrepreneurial pastors. You just have to have the right leaders around you. A plurality of elders is a beautiful thing. None of us is meant to be self-sufficient, and my fellow leaders have filled out the many gaps in my own experience and instincts.

> "You can lead a church plant and not be an entrepreneur. But you shouldn't lead a church plant if you're not a pastor."

But my personal experience is almost beside the point. Being wired as an entrepreneur is not necessary first and foremost because God doesn't say that it is. An entrepreneurial spirit isn't on any list of biblical qualifications. It can certainly be helpful in a church planting context, but any advantage is prudential, not biblical.

You can lead a church plant and not be an entrepreneur. But you shouldn't lead a church plant if you're not a pastor.

After all, "church plant" is itself a bit of a misnomer. It's a statement about chronology, not ontology. Church plants are churches, and churches don't ultimately need entrepreneurs. They need pastors. They need someone to teach them the Bible, to counsel them toward lives worthy of the gospel, to equip them for their ministry to each other.

Of course, in frontier settings, some people need to go from place-to-place starting new churches, like Paul did. Maybe that's what God has called you to. But one of Paul's top priorities was securing pastors for the churches he planted (Acts 14:23; Titus 1:5). And in the meantime, both face-to-face and through his letters, he did the work of a pastor himself.

TWO QUESTIONS FOR ENTREPRENEURIAL TYPES

If you're drawn to church planting because of your entrepreneurial itch, because you enjoy the thought of a fresh start with new challenges, you'll be vulnerable to a unique set of dangers. Here are a couple questions you should consider before you take up this work.

Why do you want to plant a church?

Entrepreneurs see opportunities in market gaps. They recognize some unmet need, some untapped demand, and they figure out how to fill the void. For some entrepreneurs, what the gap happens to be is less important than the fact that there's a gap. One writer for Forbes.com says the entrepreneur is driven by "a primordial urge, independent of product, service, industry or market." They're not necessarily more drawn to one product than any other. They just love the opportunity to start something in uncharted space.

But that motive will never be enough in healthy church planting. Instead, you must be driven by a love for local churches and the specific work of leading one. If your primary motive

> "If your primary motive is the thrill of a new venture, you'll probably struggle with the mundane, long-term work your church will need, the sort of work that is the essence of pastoral ministry."

is the thrill of a new venture, you'll probably struggle with the mundane, long-term work your church will need, the sort of work that is the essence of pastoral ministry.

You'll need to give in-depth attention to the details of people's lives. Those people may not show much progress for a long time. They may not submit quickly or easily to your counsel. But this is the work of pastoral ministry in any healthy church. Perseverance over the long term, if God allows, is the path to the greatest fruit in the lives of your people; it's also the path to your deepest joy.

What makes your new church necessary?

I've said that entrepreneurs see opportunities in market gaps. They develop and then offer products that aren't available yet. That's true in church planting, too. But we must be careful how we identify both the gap and the product we want to offer.

The only good reason to plant a church is that a specific geographical area needs more healthy churches than it already has. By "healthy church" I mean a weekly gathering where people hear and respond to God's Word on his terms. I mean a community that brings God glory by the quality of its life together. A culture where each person takes responsibility for the discipleship of others, and where that discipleship equips and mobilizes people for ministry where God has placed them. What healthy churches share, in every time and place, is far more important than any contextual features they don't share.

If the gap you want to fill is more specific than the healthy local church-in-general, if it's about some innovative approach to ministry you bring to the table, then you'll probably emphasize things the Bible hasn't prescribed and God hasn't promised to bless. And if your goal is to set your new church apart from the church down the street, then you're going to risk divisiveness.

You may also face another temptation on this front: you may see yourself as the unique product the market is missing, the object of its untapped demand. The Oxford English Dictionary online offers one sub-category to its definition of entrepreneur: "a promoter in the entertainment industry." My sense is this shade of meaning may be there, at least under the surface, when we insist that a church planter must also be an entrepreneur. We may believe that what a church plant needs to be successful is the right front-man, a charismatic personality as the face of the church.

But if you're the product you choose to promote, then you're entering a lose-lose scenario. If you fail, you'll have no one else to blame—and if your church takes off because of you, you'll have built it on something other than biblical community. You will have won glory for yourself, not for God.

Credit for the success of any church plant is a zero-sum game. After all, if we're to be faithful church planters, we must agree with John the Baptist: "He must increase; I must decrease" (John 3:30).

Matt McCullough is the pastor of Edgefield Church in Nashville, Tennessee.

Five Trends in Church Planting

by Phil Newton
and Matt Rogers

W hat makes something a trend in one season and a norm in another? While identifying trends is valuable for assessing how church planting (CP) practices work in real-life settings, trends need not be foundational. Trends should become norms only when they arise from biblical roots.

With that in mind, let's think about five trends (among many) circulating in the CP world.

1. KINGDOM OVER CHURCH

Church planters like visionary-sounding aphorisms. "Transform the city." "Advance the kingdom." "Build the kingdom." Elevated language around cooperative work has its place, yet let's make sure such language doesn't tamper with our theology. We don't "transform" the city or "build" the kingdom. The Spirit does.

> "Trends should become norms only when they arise from biblical roots."

While Jesus calls people to the kingdom (Mark 1:15), he focuses his building work on the church (Matt. 16:18). He makes his redeemed people a kingdom of priests who exercise their priestly role through local churches (Rev. 1:6).

The kingdom is amorphous, while local churches experience concrete difficulties. It's easy to talk about building the kingdom when one doesn't have a gauge for what the building will look like. It's harder to talk about planting a church where there's little gospel presence. Big ideas with lots of talk cannot be seen, but local churches—with all their weaknesses and joys—can.

It's not that kingdom language has no place. It's helpful for us to think beyond the confines of an association of churches. Plus, we need to avoid the hubris that makes us think the Lord depends on our own convention or network or denomination to accomplish the Great Commission.

"Kingdom-mindedness" means we're not just thinking about our small geographical outline but about the Lord's global work. Kingdom language looks at the church's catholicity, so that those holding firmly to "Christ alone" work together in kingdom work. With ecclesiological differences, we may not plant together, but we can cooperate and encourage, recognizing that the church is far bigger than what we can imagine.

In short, we should strive to be kingdom-minded, not to "build" the kingdom—which Jesus never entrusted to the church.

2. NETWORKS AND DENOMINATIONS

Forming subgroups of like-minded churches beyond the big tent of denominations has accelerated in CP in the past twenty years. Church planters recognize we can accomplish far more by cooperating in church planting networks than we can through bureaucracies or soloing. But cooperation requires doctrinal and methodological like-mindedness. Otherwise, we find ourselves fighting against one another, even in denominational circles where we can disagree over what constitutes *healthy* ecclesiology.

Differences of ecclesiology more broadly allow Baptists like the two of us to cooperate with Presbyterians on social action, evangelistic crusades, Bible conferences, and other disciple-making events, but not on planting a church. Planting a church requires agreeing on membership, the ordinances, and church governance. There's no use planting a church only to let confusion reign.

But networks and denominations have challenges, too. Denominations can be inefficient. Networks can revolve around one man and his way of doing church. When such men assume an apostolic leadership style without modeling humble shepherding work, they obscure or even abandon the New

Testament practice (see John 21:15–19; 1 Pet. 5:1–4).

Local churches interested in planting should seek out the wisdom and "best practices" offered by the experience of other churches. Networks and denominations can serve this purpose. Yet before joining a network or denomination, churches should consider that group's soteriological and ecclesiological priorities, as well as what practices they require for church planters.

3. IF IT DOESN'T WORK...

The Church Growth Movement (CGM) beginning in the 1960s influenced the entire direction of evangelical church planting. Donald McGavran's sociological principles for church growth, echoed and expanded by Peter Wagner, shaped denominations and their CP agencies. Church growth was equated to church health, paving a pragmatic path. Unquestionably, pragmatism has harmed the church. Churches exploded in growth but then declined almost as quickly so that once-massive churches are now shadows of themselves. Medium-to-smaller churches have worn themselves out on the CGM treadmill. And genuine conversion and discipleship have suffered in churches of every size.

Many church planters have witnessed what CGM-styled pragmatism has done to churches and want to avoid it. But where do they go? Too much CP-training leans into pragmatism, even if it goes by another name. As one who studied church growth with Wagner at Fuller Seminary, I (Phil) find it alarming to see the same CGM strategies given new terminology and repackaged for modern-day church planters. Reading Aubrey Malphurs' *Planting Growing Churches* is a case in point. It's not that he has no wisdom to offer, but much of the book is pragmatism, with some of his language simply couched differently than McGavran and Wagner.

There is a place for planters to be pragmatic, but the only way to avoid pragmatism is to emphasize biblical ecclesiology and soteriology. When considering CP literature or programming, planters should ask:

i.   Is this material biblically and hermeneutically sound?
ii. Does this material center on the gospel?
iii. Once this church is planted, who will get the glory by these methods? Will a personality, agency, denomination, or network be elevated on a pedestal due to the use of their methods? Does success rely on a program for reverse engineering results or on "the foolishness of preaching to save those who believe" (1 Cor. 1:21)?

4. CITIES AND THE MISSING MIDDLE

Most church planting work funnels personnel and resources to high-need, high-population areas. From a business standpoint, that makes good sense. But CP is not a business. That doesn't mean we should cast care to the wind, ignoring good sense and wise stewardship. But it does mean thinking counter-culturally.

We want to see people from every tribe, tongue, people, and nation follow Jesus (Rev. 5:9–10; 7:9–10). Internationally, some people belong to small people groups of a few hundred (e.g., the Yoran in Japan or Tuerke in Kyrgyzstan). Do we neglect them to focus on the Hausas or Tajiks? Domestically, there is a massive need for urban church planting, but that does not mean suburbs and small towns have already reached gospel-saturation. We want to reach all of them. Hence, we must sometimes train, send, and fund work in smaller places among smaller population units.

Perhaps sending churches lack planting-pastors, training, funds, and core teams. Then seek the Lord about how to steward what he has given you. Strategies for CP work must arise from praying to discern the will of God. Not every church planting pastor is equipped to do urban church planting. Not every team can relocate to a small town. Resources may be thin for one area but more than sufficient for another. How has the Lord provided? As you pray, you may find the Lord directing you to plant in a place the strategists have not considered. Also ask the Lord to give you discernment over planters, teams, training, and resources.

Also, read Stephen Witmer's *A Big Gospel in Small Places* and Mez McConnell and Mike McKinley's *Church in Hard Places* when you're thinking about planting counter-culturally.

5. QUICK STARTS AND SHORT-SIGHTEDNESS

Despite all the good intentions in church planting, plenty of planting pastors flame out. Energy and resources funneled into their work—sufficient or not—mean little when planters fail to hang around long enough to see a church solidify. What causes flame-outs? Often, the planter lacks the maturity to pastor people. It's not that he lacks vision, entrepreneurial skills, or a magnetic personality. It's that he lacks the spiritual strength to persevere in faithful shepherding.

How does this happen? Churches readily accept an enthusiastic potential planter but fail to properly vet or equip him for the work. They rightly want to be a sending church, but the leadership moves too quickly. They don't insist on character and competence like Paul insists on them (1 Tim. 3; Titus 1), and the prospective planter himself is captured by a sense of glamor.

If your church feels a burden to plant, don't just shove the accelerator to the floor. Speed up slowly and steadily, with discernment and patience. Get to know a man as a church member. Does he bear fruit apart from any official position? What does his discipleship to Christ look like? Wisely examining a man over time allows sending churches to recognize whether he has the character and commitment necessary for the patient work of pastoring. We're not looking for men who like the tag, "I'm a church planter." We want

> "Trends come and go. Faithful men of God committed to shepherding the local church endure."

pastors who plant with the goal to labor and solidify a church (Eph. 4:11–16; Col. 1:28–29).

Trends come and go. Faithful men of God committed to shepherding the local church endure.

Phil A. Newton is director of pastoral care & mentoring for the Pillar Network after serving 44 years as a senior pastor.

Matt Rogers is a pastor of Christ Fellowship Cherrydale in Greenville, South Carolina, assistant professor of North American Church Planting at Southeastern Baptist Theological Seminary, and resource and fundraising coordinator for The Pillar Network.

What 9Marks Purists Should Know About Church Planting

by Ed Stetzer

W hen Jonathan Leeman asked me to write an article for this issue, he sent the title above saying, "C'mon, don't you love the title?"

You see, he knows (and Mark Dever knows as well) that I love gospel clarity and biblical ecclesiology, but I'm concerned about the anti-practical nature we sometimes see in the 9Marks community.

This article is not in my place, but rather in yours, at their request, because they know I share so much in common. As a matter of fact, the last few churches I planted all used Dever's *A Display of God's Glory* to describe our polity. But I do think that there are some issues to consider in church planting. So, I've created nine things that 9Marks purists should know, because nine is a holy number!

1. Preaching does not plant churches.

Your preaching is not as important as you think it is, at least in church planting.

Now, don't be a hater yet—keep in mind that this is a conversation about church planting. Let me be clear, preaching the Scriptures exegetically and theologically accurately is essential, meaningful, and vital to the health of your church, but it is not the first thing you do. You must also build relationships, share the gospel, and start groups.

You evangelize a church into existence, and then you start preaching to the church of the newly evangelized.

Yes, preaching and teaching are marks of a biblical church, but it is not how you plant a church. Preaching is a part of how you pastor a church— but you have to plant it (through evangelism) first.

Now, if you start with a group being sent out, and it's already a functioning church, that's another story on preaching—but it's the same story on evangelism. Evangelism has to be a driver if it really is church planting and not just hiving off a new preaching point.

Too many purists love preaching more than planting (and sometimes more than people), leading to a "plant" that is usually more about people wanting better and more Reformed preaching.

> "Evangelism has to be a driver if it really is church planting and not just hiving off a new preaching point."

2. Practical ministry and pragmatism are not the same thing.

Never plant a church in your head.

For theorists and theologians, there is a danger of adopting methodology and modes of church planting without understanding their specific culture or context. We need a vision for the people God is calling us to, which means we must know them and then develop practical steps to actually plant a church among them. These practical steps can be as simple as meeting every neighbor on your street, inviting people to come with you to church, attending community events, and so on. Church planting can't stay in the clouds, it has to make the practical jump to the streets.

And what you heard in a conference or in seminary is not always the same as it is practically applied and lived out when you are planting from the inner city to the rural farmland.

3. You plant by engaging the lost, not by immersing yourself in church culture.

You cannot live and love like Jesus without spending significant time with the people who don't know him.

Jesus said he came to "seek and save the lost" (Luke 19:10), and we are called to join him on his mission. As a church planter, it's surprising that making and protecting time to spend with people who need to hear about Jesus is difficult, but it is. It can be easy to drift into the mode of teaching others fantastic methodology on seeking out those who are lost but spend little time modeling it ourselves. This can create a church of intellectually well-equipped yet completely inexperienced missionaries. As church planters, with the various demands on your time, you must viciously protect the time you spend with friends, neighbors, and co-workers (if you're bi-vocational) who don't yet know Jesus. Modeling this, and doing it together with members of your church plant, will mold your culture around mission.

For a lot of purists, they have immersed themselves in a church or religious culture. Have you ever noticed how easy it is for us to start saying spiritually sounding phrases around people who are not spiritually inclined? That's a sign of church culture, not biblical truth, and of not knowing and engaging with normal people.

4. Cultural engagement is both crucial and not natural for the theologically inclined.

You want to be both theologically astute and culturally engaged in order to plant a church effectively.

Sometimes, the people who are more adept at cultural engagement tend to be less theologically inclined, but that is not always a correlation. Often those who have studied theology for years find themselves missing cultural context clues, and their preaching is distant and disparate.

Planting a church well involves exegeting the culture that God has sovereignly placed you in. This takes time, energy, effort, and intentionality. We must preach Christ and the Scriptures with a faithful understanding of theology, but we must also communicate in the language and cultural context of our time. I find it ironic that those who love the Puritans sometimes betray the Puritan practice of "speaking plainly."

You can be and should be both engaged in culture and theologically driven in your approach to ministry.

5. You won't preach and disciple your way to evangelism. You must lead your church TO evangelism by engaging IN evangelism WITH them.

It is a myth that preaching and teaching will always produce an evangelistic church. It often doesn't.

Good teaching in isolation rarely has a transformative effect, though people tell me all the time that's their plan. A preacher's sermons must be matched by the activities of his life (1 Tim. 4:16; 2 Tim. 3:10). Watching you actively attend to your own and their evangelism, pastor, is the illustration your sermons need to create a new culture. Evangelism needs to be caught and taught.

I actually had a discussion with one 9Marks purist (did I mention that was Jonathan's phrase?) about that very thing. He was frustrated that he was teaching and preaching, discipling and going deeper, but evangelism was not increasing.

He agreed to do whatever I suggested for a few months. So, we planned outreach days, started a new series that was easy for Christians to bring guests

> "It is a myth that preaching and teaching will always produce an evangelistic church. It often doesn't."

(and then planned a bring-a-friend emphasis), planned church-wide outreach into the community, organized a prayer strategy, and more.

The end result? He did nothing that violated his purist views (that was our deal), yet soon the church was growing because it was mobilized and God was blessing.

6. You can learn from people who are reaching people.

I often tell people that if they want to get a bad reputation for their church, start growing. Pastors who lead churches that aren't growing will find ways to explain away other churches' growth as illegitimate.

Yes, there are false converts. Yes, there are bad methodologies. No, we don't want to be momentum-dependent. But maybe you can learn more by asking, "What can I learn from someone who is reaching people that I am not reaching?"

7. Love Jesus.

8. Preach the gospel.

9. Care about ecclesiology.

OK, I assumed we all would agree on the last three. And I wanted you to know that I'm with you on so much.

When Mark and I discussed this one day, I told him (in, I hope, a nice way) I believed he was creating a whole generation of theologically minded but practically uninformed pastors that are less effective than they could be.

He responded something like, they are reading all the practical books (and he graciously said many of them were mine). However, I am not convinced that is always the case. (And, Mark, your books sell a whole lot more than mine.)

But, in his answer, I found my hope. Mark is assuming you are getting the practical from somewhere. My concern is that 9Marks purists are not—and they need to.

So, learn best practices, learn how to engage the lost, learn how to lead your church well to engage its community, but don't do so by moving away from the gospel, the Scriptures, and a biblical understanding of church.

That's my exhortation to you . . . my friends, 9Marks purists!

Ed Stetzer is the Dean of Talbot School of Theology at Biola University and Scholar in Residence & Teaching Pastor at Mariners Church.

Section Two

Sending Out a Church Plant

Taking Risks in Church Planting by Sending Your Best Members and Elders

by Juan Sanchez

66 **I**f you had to do it all over again, would you still do it?"

That sounds like a question you might ask someone who's just been convicted of a crime, and it's one I was asked just this morning. My crime? Sending off 37 of our best members, along with two of our best elders, to plant a church. The prosecutor? An elder of a brand-new church plant in Dubai. I had just shared with him how much our latest church plant cost us.

We can always find reasons, even good ones, for not planting a church. And yet, the need for church planting in my town (Austin, Texas) far outweighs whatever adverse effects we may face.

OUR NEED TO PLANT ANOTHER CHURCH

We didn't need to plant another church because we were bursting at the seams. We still have plenty of room in our building.

We didn't plant another church because we possess abundant financial resources. We have an overwhelming debt that hangs like a millstone around our necks.

Instead, we needed to plant a church for pastoral and evangelistic reasons.

First, we had a significant number of members who were driving from northwest Austin to gather with us each week. That's at least a thirty-minute drive for most of them. When members live that far away, it's hard to "shepherd the flock of God among you" (1 Pet. 5:2). We struggled to foster gospel community among our membership because distance became a logistical obstacle.

Second, those members who lived far away found it hard to build gospel relationships with neighbors and invite them to our gatherings.

But not only did we need to plant a church, our city needed us to plant another church. Between 2005 and 2015, metro Austin grew by almost 38 percent, surpassing two million people. In fact, from July 1, 2015 to July 1, 2016, the metro Austin population increased by 58,301. That's about 164 people per day. Such growth means church planting efforts in our city aren't keeping up with population growth. In our context, we cannot afford NOT to plant a church.

OUR CALCULATED RISK IN PLANTING ANOTHER CHURCH

So then, understanding our pastoral and evangelistic concerns, and our city's need, we took a calculated risk and planted another church. There is almost

> "No matter the costs and effects of church planting on the planting church, the Lord is always faithful."

never a good time to plant a church. You can almost always find valid, even logical reasons for putting it off. In our case, though, we realized that many of our reasons for not planting were grounded in fear. We were afraid of losing members, finances, and leaders.

And we felt the effects of planting a church almost immediately. Previously, we had eight elders for just over 500 members. The December before we planted, one of our elders rotated off the elder board. In February of the following year, our new church plant held their first public meetings. In a period of just over two months we went from eight elders to five. And once the church plant officially received new members, we removed those we had sent from our membership: a total of 37.

Don't get me wrong. We weren't just interested in the numbers. But those numbers represented some of our best members and strongest givers. Consequently, over the next year we began to feel the void. Our five remaining elders found it hard to care for our almost 500 members. Though we reduced our new budget by ten percent to account for the calculated loss in income, our giving wasn't as strong as we'd hoped. At this point, planting that new church seemed like a foolish decision.

So, if we had to do it again, would we still do it? Absolutely!

THE BLESSINGS OF PLANTING A CHURCH

As always, God is faithful. When we sent off 37 of our best members in February 2015, we asked God to send us 37 new members over the next year. The Lord answered our prayers. He caused the growth (1 Cor. 3:6), and by the end of 2015, we had received 74 new members. As we observed God's kindness, we were encouraged in our decision to plant a church. Had we not planted a new church, we would have missed out on the joy of answered prayer for new members.

Unfortunately, the addition of new members didn't offset our financial deficit. We thought reducing our budget by ten percent, along with new member growth, would address our financial needs. We were wrong.

But again, God is faithful! Several months into the life of the new church plant, they had more money than we did. Understanding our financial situation, they asked us to stop providing them with financial support. Though we rejoiced in their financial freedom and were thankful for their generosity, that financial relief was not enough to keep our church from financial hardship. By the fall of our new church plant's second year, we found ourselves in a significant financial deficit.

We were approximately $130,000 behind our budget. After much deliberation, our elders agreed to go before the congregation and let them know of our need. In addition to our normal weekly need of about $28,000, the elders proposed a one-day special offering with a $100,000 goal. By God's grace, our members responded

> "the Lord has taught us that not only does our city need us to keep planting churches, but, for the health of our church, we need to keep planting churches."

in overflowing generosity. We received just over $105,000 for the special offering, and about $48,000.00 for our regular weekly offering. Had we not planted a new church, we would never have known God's grace through the generosity of our members (2 Cor. 8:1–5).

Finally, we still had a need for more leaders (2 Tim. 2:2). Because of the burden of so few elders caring for so many members, we asked God for more elders. As always, we continued identifying elder-qualified men in the congregation. But now, we sensed a greater urgency. Having prayed regularly and tested men diligently, we identified several younger men in our congregation who were qualified. One year after planting the church, the elder that had previously rotated off returned, bringing us to six elders. We also identified another five men we believed were qualified. Though for various reasons two of those men were unable to serve at that time, three of them were. Over that next year, the church affirmed all three of them, and, as of today, we have nine elders. Had we not planted a church, we may not have moved on these men with urgency, but each of these brothers has proven to be a valuable addition to our eldership.

CONCLUSION

There is no question in my mind that we would do it all over again. In fact, we did it again in 2022. We sent out 47 members, including two elders and two men who were in our own elder pipeline. And with them went about $140,000 of our annual budget. This is now our fifth church plant. And every time, there is a cost. But every time we see the Lord's faithfulness in sustaining us.

To be sure, not every context is the same. Not every town is growing like Austin. Not every church will be blessed in the same ways. But, after planting these churches, the Lord has taught us that not only does our city need us to keep planting churches, but, for the health of our church, we need to keep planting churches. And that would be true whether or not we continue to grow, increase our budget, and raise an abundance of new leaders. No matter the costs and effects of church planting on the planting church, the Lord is always faithful.

Juan Sanchez is the senior pastor of High Pointe Baptist Church in Austin, Texas. You can find him on Twitter at @manorjuan.

Should I Stay or Should I Go? Advice for Members on Church Plants

by John Joseph

I magine with me that you're at your church's weekly prayer service. After making a few mundane announcements, the pastor preps the congregation for big news—big news that has been in the works for some time.

"We're planting a church!" he says triumphantly. Excited gasps erupt. Applause and cheers break out. Then, when the excitement dies down, the questions from the congregation come. "Who will the pastor be?" "Where will the church be planted?" "Where will the church meet?"

You—because you're a fan of the rock band *The Clash*—hear in your mind that iconic opening guitar riff, and you stand and ask in your best Joe Strummer voice, "Pastor, you gotta let me know, should I stay or should I go?"

If your church plants a church, that's one of the most important questions you should ask. Should you remain at the church you're a member of or should you join in this new work?

The answer to that question isn't always clear. It often includes weighing numerous competing factors and simply trying to make the most informed decision possible. There are times, however, where the circumstances of a situation make the decision easier. Let me offer four clear reasons why you should consider *not* joining a new church plant.

1. YOU'RE IN A BAD PLACE SPIRITUALLY

You generally shouldn't join a church plant if you're struggling spiritually. By struggling spiritually, I don't mean you feel spiritually dry, or you aren't as consistent in your quiet times as you would like to be, or even that you feel like you're playing whack-a-mole with sin in your life.

What I mean is that you're in a place of needing acute pastoral care. This might look like a married couple on the brink of separation. It could look like a single man battling substance abuse. It might look like a college girl struggling terribly with depression. The list of potential scenarios is endless.

If you're in need of regular, acute pastoral care, you should consider not joining a church plant for two reasons. First, you benefit from the continuity of care. Staying at your church will enable pastors familiar with your situation to provide the care and support you will need as you work through whatever difficult circumstances you're facing.

Second, in the beginning stages of a church plant, pastors are often unable to provide the acute care people need.

Have you ever heard of the phrase "death by a thousand paper cuts"? Nowhere is that phrase truer than in planting a church.

In most church plants, the pastor isn't just the pastor. He's also the church administrator, events coordinator, website designer, facility manager, lead deacon, lone small group leader, and community liaison; not to mention also often a husband and father. Burnout, anyone?

Don't get me wrong, pastors of church plants should expect to pastor their members through all sorts of difficult circumstances. It's just that in the beginning stages of a church plant, they will likely be unable to provide the acute care you'll need if you're struggling spiritually.

2. YOU'RE DOING REALLY WELL SPIRITUALLY

You should also consider not joining a church plant if you're prospering spiritually. I'm talking "crushing the game" level prospering. Not your run-of-the-mill, "Yeah, I'm doing well spiritually, I guess," type of prospering.

Your knowledge of the Word is growing in ways you haven't experienced before. The Lord is blessing your discipling relationships. You're joyfully taking on greater responsibility in your church, and the church is benefitting as a result. Your life—by God's grace—looks like a fruit farm at harvest time.

Recognize that seasons of spiritual prosperity are gifts from God. If you're in a season like that, praise God! Also, don't interrupt the work by moving on from the circumstances in which he's doing it. These unique seasons don't last forever. Be a sponge and soak up all the good that God is doing in your life so that you can be wrung out for the good of others at some point in the future.

3. YOU CAN'T ENVISION SITTING UNDER THE PROSPECTIVE PASTOR'S PREACHING

If you're considering joining a church plant, one of the most important questions you need to ask yourself is, "Can I envision sitting under this particular pastor's preaching each week? And what about my family or any non-Christians I might bring to church?" In an ideal world, we would all love to listen to and benefit equally from every pastor who faithfully preaches God's Word.

> "If you're considering joining a church plant, one of the most important questions you need to ask yourself is, 'Can I envision sitting under this particular pastor's preaching each week? And what about my family or any non-Christians I might bring to church?'"

Unfortunately, we don't live in an ideal world, so we won't all benefit equally from every pastor who faithfully preaches God's Word. Some people prefer more cerebral preaching, while others prefer more down-to-earth preaching. Some appreciate emotionally restrained preaching, while others appreciate emotionally expressive preaching. Some people want 60-minute sermons, while others want 30-minute sermons. Sometimes you just don't like the way a certain preacher sounds.

If you think you'll struggle to sit under the prospective pastor's preaching, you should consider staying put.

4. YOU DISAGREE WITH THE PROSPECTIVE PASTOR ON ENOUGH SECONDARY MATTERS

Finally, if you disagree with the prospective pastor on enough secondary matters (or other important issues), then you should not consider joining. Secondary matters have historically been matters along which denominational lines have been drawn, but even within the same denomination there can be disagreement over how particular secondary doctrines are applied.

For example, Baptists agree that only believers should be baptized, but they may disagree over when a person should be baptized or who should be admitted to the Lord's Table. But beyond secondary matters, there are a whole host of other important issues like polity, the role of women in the church, divorce and remarriage, spiritual gifts, the church and social justice, and many more that a prospective pastor will have to take a position on.

If you find that you disagree on enough of those issues, then you should consider staying at your current church. And I'm saying "enough" because I don't think disagreement on just one necessarily prevents you from joining. If, however, you find that there are numerous secondary matters and/or important issues that you disagree on, then that's a good sign you should not join that church plant.

John Joseph is the pastor of Cheverly Baptist Church in Cheverly, Maryland.

Sending Out Future Leaders Strategically

by Matt Rogers

Ask most kids what they want to be when they grow up, and they'll tell you: Astronaut. Storm chaser. Lego maker. It's cute, but not realistic.

Ask seminarians or young leaders in the church this question, and they'll fumble through some possible scenarios. Plant a church. Revitalize a dying church. Pastor an established congregation. Many just aren't sure where and how their gifts are most suited for the work.

Pastors developing future leaders can help using these seven diagnostic questions. In so doing, they will send future leaders more strategically.

1. Is he a pastor or does he like the thought of being a pastor?

This is *the* question. We must always start here. Every future pastor must first meet the biblical qualifications for the character and competence of one who is entrusted with leadership in the church (1 Tim. 3:1–7; Titus 1:3–7; 1 Pet. 5:1–11). What is a church planter if not a pastor of God's people? What is a church revitalizer, re-planter, established church pastor if not one entrusted to shepherd the flock of God?

In many ways, the stark dichotomy between church planting and revitalization creates a distinction that confuses rather than helps. Both planters and revitalizers must aspire to the qualifications of the office of pastor and not merely some form of the work they believe fits their gifts or abilities.

So start here. Force future leaders to grapple with the hard work of character development. See if they possess a genuine love for the people of God. Watch how they invest as meaningful members of the church. Allow pastors to distinguish themselves as pastors before you put them in subcategories of ways they can deploy their pastoral function.

2. Is he more effective at making something from nothing or taking something and making it better?

Once we know we have a pastor, then we can talk about specialization. It's true that some pastors are better church planters, others better revitalizers, and still others better at stepping into a relatively healthy, established church. This shouldn't suggest that an effective planter could not also revitalize, or that one apt in revitalization might not be able to plant a church. But it's wise to consider how best to deploy the dominant strength of those we send.

Planters start with nothing—no systems, no structure, no people—and build from scratch. Some pastors enjoy the freedom, creativity, and faith that this work requires. Revitalizers, on the other hand, step into something that is broken and bring structure, order, and health. Those with this leaning tend to find joy in the patient toil required to identify the problems, build unity, and redirect energy.

The best way to discern which of these fits a future leader is to look at the track record of his life and see where he's experienced joy and seen fruit in the past. If past ministry doesn't give indication, then the current church provides a context for experimentation. Give future leaders something that is broken and see what they do with it or give them a vision for something that doesn't exist and see if they can bring it to life.

3. Does he relate better with insiders or outsiders?

It's not *if* pastors will have to lead with vision, but *with whom* they should start in casting a vision.

Pastors leading established churches toward health will start with an existing nucleus of church attendees. These people may or may not be Christians. They may not be invested meaningfully in God's mission. Depending on the degree of dysfunction, they've likely been hurt by past leaders and may have attached themselves to the organization of the church and not its mission. These pastors will step into this maze of complexity and compel some of these people to redirect their energy to a new vision for the church's future. They will also cast vision that causes some to opt-out and go elsewhere.

In contrast, church planters start with new relationships. While they may have a church planting team or some early adopters who are believers, these people are far less connected than generational members of an established church. Often church planters will start with non-believers who come to faith and give themselves to the mission. Other times, they will invest in immature Christians who've never been discipled and see little value in the church. Who's drawn to the vision of this leader is a key indicator of where he will thrive.

4. Does he have genuine love for senior saints?

There's a difference in whether a future leader *can* be patient with older Christians or whether he truly finds joy in such work.

Patient toil with senior saints will not be optional for revitalizers and established church pastors. They will step into a role where these members are normative. Many may have generational connections to the church. Anyone capable of bringing health to a church will have to engage in the laborious work of fostering relationships, cultivating trust, and giving care to these senior saints.

Planters, on the other hand, have a different challenge when it comes to senior saints. Intentionally or unintentionally, many church plants are comprised of young, early adopters. For a vibrant, multigenerational ministry to take root, however, the church must retain senior saints willing to take a risk in a new congregation. To do so, planters will need to develop the skill of fostering new relationships with both Christians and non-Christians who are much older than them and have no long-standing commitment to the church—or to any church for that matter. It's not that planters will not need to love senior saints, but they will often be starting from a different place in the relationship.

5. Can he handle a lack of fruit for a season?

A planter will have a lengthy season of sowing gospel seed through evangelism, during which time he may not see a single convert. He will often not have a building or a budget. There won't be staff or ministry programs for a time. In the early years, a planting pastor must be able to live with the reality that this whole deal could really fall apart tomorrow.

A revitalizer, on the other hand, may inherit a shell of buildings, structures, and programs that could exist for years in the same state of disrepair. The generational solidity of the church likely means that the church isn't going away tomorrow. But the revitalizer will likely have extended seasons of fruitlessness as well. It takes time to build trust, to earn the right to lead in a new place. The labor to share the gospel and integrate new members into the church will not happen overnight. Purging the membership, installing elders, and streamlining programs all take time.

A future leader is picking his challenge. Where can he best handle the complexity of fruitlessness?

6. How did he fall in love with the church?

Don't underestimate the future leader's story in considering where he best fits. Consider where he developed a love for the church and leverage God's past work to press into future ministry.

For example, a young man who came to faith and grew to love the church through a church plant near his university may long to replicate that work in another place. In contrast, a man who came to faith through a century-old, established church may be drawn to invest in the work of restoring those types of churches to health.

In the same way, we tend to give care to others who've experienced some of the same pain we have—addicts are drawn to other addicts, the divorced to those in hard marriages, widows to other widows—future leaders are often best suited for a type of ministry birthed out of their story.

7. What opportunities are before you?

Churches should consider what kind of strengths a man might have. Yet they should also simply think about where needs and opportunities exist. Sometimes, the answers we give to the previous six questions might suggest that a man will do best ministering one kind of way. But we're not all-wise. God is.

Maybe a nearby church has fallen on hard times and needs a pastor, and maybe the only person whose life circumstances would enable him and his family to go is someone your church had slotted as a would-be planter. No doubt, we should consider how a person's gifts are best deployed. But as Christ's servants, pastors are pastors, and every one of us should be willing to leverage our lives for the sake of God's glory among his people in his church in whatever form they are needed.

After all, who you are (pastor) and what you are leading (God's church) is far more important than where you do the work.

Matt Rogers is a pastor of Christ Fellowship Cherrydale in Greenville, South Carolina, assistant professor of North American Church Planting at Southeastern Baptist Theological Seminary, and resource and fundraising coordinator for The Pillar Network.

Equipping Women for Church Planting

by Sharon Dickens

A s I sat and scanned the faces of the women before me, I leaned back and smiled to myself. There sat a mix of female interns, apprentices, women's workers, and ministry wives—all church plant core team members who were poised and ready to be taught this week's session from our women's ministry curriculum. It was glorious.

In the last fifteen years, I've been both amazed and frustrated as I've seen the global conversation on women's ministry slowly move beyond the usual dialogue into action.

In the book *Women's Ministry in the Local Church*, Ligon Duncan writes, "Some church leaders are so afraid of women assuming unbiblical roles in the church *that they fail to equip them for the roles to which they have been indisputably called in the home and the church.*"[1]

I have reflected on Ligon Duncan's quote many times, wondering if this perpetual cycle of debate was in some way fueled by the paralyzing "fear" he identified. What has all this inaction cost?

Mez McConnell said, "The pastor is not seen as the only one who is qualified to minister among the flock he shepherds. That is a good thing, as one man cannot adequately take on this role. Even with a small church and multiple elders, we would struggle under the weight of pastoral issues in our congregation. Women . . . have a serious part to play in the kingdom of God. . . . They are not just bystanders."[2]

Equipping women *well* and releasing them to serve surely benefits the home and church. Thankfully, I feel the tide turning as the tone of the discussion has started to change from "should we" to "how do we?" Even the existence of this article testifies to the shift. How do I tackle such an important topic? After much reflection, I want to highlight just three simple, yet foundational points.

Dispel the Myth of Longevity Equaling Maturity

Sometimes I'm like a broken record. One of my favorite recurring phrases is "Old doesn't mean mature." Sadly, we mistake the length of faith as some sort of measurement for maturity. This isn't just a women's issue; it's a church member's issue. Some who have been Christians for a long time are sadly immature. They might be a walking concordance and can quote Scripture and verse, but it turns out they are merely speakers of the Word and not doers.

The key to *equipping well* is to ensure you pick well in the first place. Think beyond the obvious usual

> "the key to equipping well is to ensure you pick well in the first place."

suspects and watch out for those who show potential, are servant-hearted, and are teachable. You may even have to dispel your own presuppositions of the legendary "Proverbs 31" woman. She is quite literally proverbial. I repeat, the key to *equipping well* is to ensure you *pick well* in the first place.

Get the Structure Right

I recently wrote a book called Unconventional: A Practical Guide to Women's Ministry in the Local Church. I spend a lot of time trying to explain how to create a robust women's ministry that teaches and cares for the women in the church while remaining in glad submission to the elders.[3] Part of the answer is a well-thought-through structure. We have to grapple with hard questions like:

- What does confidentiality look like? When can it be broken?
- When do pastors get involved in a crisis involving sisters who are church members?
- What do we want our one-to-one discipling and evangelism framework to look like? Can women do one-on-with a man?
- What does our discipleship pathway look like? What books and study materials will we use?

- How do we prevent paternalism and dependency? Do we respond to a need with cash? How can we develop women's ministry without it becoming independent of the church?

The list of questions is endless and some answers may differ depending on your context. Some of these questions are easier to answer than others but grappling with them and finding an answer will provide the foundational structure for what your women's ministry will look like. This is key. Having a framework will equip the trained women on your core team, in time, to pass something on to the generation of women.

No one wants random church members dancing to their own tune. In fact, a lack of structure may explain why some women's ministry has previously headed in unhelpful directions. You don't need to be a structural engineer to know that if the foundational structure isn't right then the whole building's integrity is compromised. That's why building codes exist.

In some ways, all this is easier to deal with in a church plant. After all, you've got a piece of "new land" to build our foundation on and can start fresh. But whether you're in a new or established church, careful structure is vital.

In our care team, we have eight women all with their own personalities. We all work within the same structural framework so that we pass on the same framework to the next generation, but we do so in our unique way. We sing the same tune but in different keys. *Equipping well* requires you to *plan well*.

Equip and Prepare for Service

I love thinking through ways to help stretch, grow, and see women step out of their comfort zone. I love teaching women how to cope or deal with hard conversations and problems without brushing them under the carpet. I'd like to tell you we teach them something fabulous and new but, truthfully, we simply teach Titus 2:3–4. Simple, biblical, and thought-through training has three key elements: Knowledge, Character, and Practice.

Knowledge. Over the last decade, we have developed several courses for women. Our goal is to deliver biblically robust teaching in a practical way. We talk about a vast array of topics:

- how feminism has shaped our world
- biblical submission
- women in leadership
- dealing with conflict
- what to do when men won't lead

We have 22 basic sessions written and delivered by women. We teach in various ways: one-on-one, in small groups, online, in the classroom, and through books (even our own). I've been asked many times, "Can you come and train our women?" I'd love to be able to say yes, but time is limited. This encouraged us to create resources that we think can be helpful for any church. Our books *Unexceptional* and *Unconventional* each give a big-picture overview. We're passionate to get good resources into the right hands so we also have created a companion resource (*Unconventional:*

A Resource Guide). This includes all our foundational training sessions to download, tweak, and contextualize. It can be time-consuming and daunting to work through and create training to equip women. We may all learn in different ways, but we all need the same foundational information.

Character. "Search me, God, and know my heart; test me and know my anxious thoughts. See if there is any offensive way in me, and lead me in the way everlasting" (Psalm 139:23–24). Knowledge can be taught and skills can be improved, but character is a different story. As my wee mum would say: the proof is in the pudding. The Psalmist uses words like "search," "test me," and "see." I know he was addressing the Lord, but there is a foundational pattern there to help us identify and recognize spiritual growth with prayer, discernment, and wisdom. To do this, we need an intentional and intensive discipleship framework. As godly, mature women invest in, disciple, and hold young women accountable, growth will be more evident, weaknesses will be identified and challenged, and women will be urged to cling to Christ.

Practice. We live in a target-driven world where people find their identity in achievements. Our churches should cultivate an environment where people can *fail well*. After all, we all fail. Some of our best lessons come from our biggest mistakes. We all need to grow and develop the skills needed for the roles God has given us. Many capable women I know get frustrated when teaching younger Christians new tasks because they make mistakes and don't get everything right. Lots of times I hear, "I

can do it quicker and better myself!" That may be true. But if we want to help them, we can't do ministry for them. Short-term costs prepare us for long-term gains.

> "We all need experience and the opportunity to receive constructive help, even if that means we hear a few uncomfortable truths now and then."

So again: our churches should offer opportunities for those who want to do ministry, even if that means we're not always getting the "best" and most experienced people for every job. No one can excel in anything without experience. We all need experience and the opportunity to receive constructive help, even if that means we hear a few uncomfortable truths now and then. *Equipping well* requires the most experienced of you to *patiently repeat with grace* what someone needs to hear for the 100th time.

Conclusion

Recently at a conference, I was asked to highlight my take-home point. I said, "I want everyone to go away *underwhelmed* by what they hear. So underwhelmed they think, she hasn't told me anything I don't know and can't do myself." To be honest, I hope you say the same about this article. I would love you to get to this last sentence and be so underwhelmed by what you've read that you think, "This isn't rocket science. With some thought and the right women on my team, we can do this."

---

1. *Emphasis mine. Duncan, L and Hunt, S. Women's Ministry in the Local Church. (Crossway, 2006). 22.*

2. *McConnell, Mez. https://20schemesequip. com/why-my-first-church-hire-was-a-woman-and-why-yours-should-be-too/ or*

A version of this foreword appears in Mez McConnell, The Least, the Last and the Lost, *part IV, chapter 3 (EP, 2021).*

3. *Dickens, Sharon. Unconventional. A Practical Gide to Women's Ministry in the Local Church. 10Publishing, Great Britain, 2023. 17*

Sharon Dickens is the Director of Women's Ministry at 20schemes.

Shepherding the Heart in Sending

by Dave Kiehn

I was walking toward Jennifer in our sanctuary. "Pastor, can I talk to you?" she asked. I responded, "I already know." Then we both cried. I learned the day before that she felt led to be part of the core team of our new church plant.

Jennifer came to our church in college, was baptized in our congregation, served as a summer intern, and was instrumental in our church revitalization. Our family and church loved her. We were thrilled and sad. She was thrilled and sad.

How do you shepherd the hearts of those who are sent? What about those who stay? Paul charged the Ephesian elders in Acts 20:28, "Pay careful attention to yourselves and to all the flock, in which the Holy Spirit has made you overseers, to care for the church of God, which he obtained with his own blood."

We must pay careful attention to the whole flock, the sent and the senders, since both were obtained with the precious blood of Christ.

SHEPHERDING THE HEARTS OF THOSE WHO ARE SENT

Through Joy

Planting a church is exciting. People feel new energy building a new work. We must help the senders celebrate the work the Lord has done in their hearts to impel them to go.

Through Grief

Pastors need to help those being sent to deal with separation anxiety while leaving a body they love. Sadness is natural when change happens. People need to take time to reflect and rejoice in all the Lord has done in the present body. While grieving, they will no longer be a part of this congregation, but they will remain members of the same family in Christ—forever.

For Perseverance

Church planting is not easy. The shine of the *church plant's* tender young leaves dull and blooms fade. Relationships grow difficult. The inconveniences associated with church plants become tiresome. Pastors must prepare the hearts of CP team members to persevere. They must have realistic expectations of what will happen. They must understand that long and hard conversations will precede desires to return.

Transitioning Authority

It is a challenge to give away authority, but it is essential for the planting elder to assume responsibility for the core team. Sending pastors can't pull back completely but must hand off avenues of authority progressively and

with confidence. The conversations about future job decisions, the counseling of sin, corrective counsel for family issues, and the joys of praying over newborn babies will be given to another body of elders.

> "Pastors need to help those being sent to deal with separation anxiety while leaving a body they love."

Ongoing Care

Even though we have placed authority into the hands of others, it's important to check up on those you've sent. "How has the transition been? How can we pray for you? We miss you." We have sent some dear brothers and sisters whom we didn't follow up with, and it felt to them like we didn't care. I would encourage pastors to develop and maintain some mechanism to check in and care for those who are being sent. Every instance of heart-felt shepherding will deepen their love, not just for one particular local church, but for the beauty and gift of the church of Jesus Christ.

SHEPHERDING THE HEARTS OF THOSE WHO STAY

Through Grief

It is hard to send away people you love. Even though the new church may just be down the street, it will still dramatically change relationships. We need to allow our congregation to grieve the goodbyes.

Through Joy

Although sending goodbyes are bittersweet, they are also glorious. God's kingdom is advancing. We are joining in God's global mission of gospel redemption. The church should celebrate every time it hears of new work happening in our city, nation, and world.

Reinvestment

Church planting is exhausting and costly for the sending church. Many members will struggle to pour their lives into people amid seasons of transition. We must encourage and exhort our members to keep discipling one another, even if some are called to go elsewhere. Investing our lives will be worth it in this life and eternity.

> "Pastors must prepare the hearts of church planting team members to persevere in the work God has called them to."

Do It Again

Pastors must shepherd their churches to want to plant again. It is costly, time consuming, and emotionally draining, but it is worth it. Yes, we will lose some of our best. Yes, our budget will decrease. Yes, we will lose enthusiastic volunteers. Yes, Jesus and his kingdom are worth it. Let's do it again!

SHEPHERDING THE HEART OF THE SHEPHERD

Paul encouraged the Ephesian elders to pay attention to themselves too. Brothers, church planting is hard on the heart of a shepherd.

Slaying the Idol of Vainglory

Personally, planting a church has revealed so much pride and vainglory in my heart. I preached for years about rejoicing in all gospel growth in our city, even if it happened down the street. And then people decided to leave our body and go down the street to join a new work. And I struggled with it. I struggled because I had an idol of success and wanted to make a name for myself. Church planting slowly and consistently helped put to death my vainglory, and I praise God for it.

Be Ready for the Rollercoaster

It is natural to have highs and lows in the planting process. You'll get excited about people following God's will and then sad they are gone. One day, you will rejoice in the strength of the core team and, the next, struggle with fear over the budget. New visitors will choose the plant over your church. Sometimes, you'll rejoice that they are where God wants them to be; other days you'll be discouraged that "your church" wasn't chosen. Be ready for the emotional rollercoaster. Communicate with your elders while consistently confessing your sins. Wait for the Lord to move in matters and always give God the glory.

SHEPHERDING FOR THE CHIEF SHEPHERD

All our shepherding is for the glory of God. While being sensitive to your own heart, allow God to use the sending and staying to slay idols and grow you in Christ's image. The Chief Shepherd laid down his life for sheep like Jennifer, and we are to do the same.

Our church still misses Jennifer, we still pray for her, and we rejoice she is still walking with Christ. Our labors for the sheep are for God and his glory, and our pains will be worth it in this life and the life to come.

Dave Kiehn is Lead Pastor of Park Baptist Church, Rock Hill, SC.

Section Three

Planting a Church

Stop Launching Churches, Covenant Together Instead

by Nathan Knight

I think we should stop talking about "launching" new church plants and instead refer to them "covenanting" for the first time.

WHY DO WE SAY "LAUNCH"?

I am a church planter myself. I've learned from other planters, talked to planters, read updates from planters, and read the books on church planting. And we all say "launch."

Why?

I asked a few. Their responses were not all the same. The most common answer I have heard is, "This is the date on which our planting team 'goes public.'" When I follow up by asking if a person from the public could have attended their meetings before the "launch" the common answer is "sure."

> "Here's what I think
> we planters have done:
> borrowed a word from
> the business world
> in order to garner
> energy and inject life
> into a church from its
> beginning."

So what actually happened when you "launched" if people from the public could have attended before? Apparently, launching is different than having a child or getting married. You *know* when those things happen!

Here's what I think we planters have done: borrowed a word from the business world in order to garner energy and inject life into a church from its beginning.

HOW ABOUT "COVENANT" INSTEAD?

I would like to advocate the use of the biblical word "covenant" to designate the beginning of a church, as in "We first covenanted as a congregation on June 24."

You find a picture of the returning exiles renewing their covenant with each other and God in Nehemiah 9:32–38. And the fellowship of a church is a kind of covenant, whereby we affirm one another's professions of faith and agree to oversee one another's discipleship to Christ. This is the cumulative picture that you see in Matthew 16 when Jesus affirms Peter and Peter's profession (v. 17), and

that you see again (in inverse form) in Matthew 18 when the church removes its affirmation of someone's profession of faith (v. 17).

What is a church? It's a gathering of two or three people in Christ's name—a society of people covenanted together in the same gospel profession. Through baptism and the Lord's Supper we partake of this local covenant together as our localized picture of our new covenant membership. (Bobby Jamieson, in his book *Going Public*, describes baptism as the *initiating oath sign of the new covenant*. And he describes the Lord's Supper as the *renewing oath sign of the new covenant*.)

I don't think Scripture compels us to use the word "covenanting" to speak about the beginning of a church. It doesn't tell us we must. I'm not saying that either. I do think the word helpfully captures what happens in Scripture when a group of Christians organize as a church. Therefore I'm offering it as a "best practice."

NOT JUST TRADING ONE WORD FOR ANOTHER

"Covenanting" is more than just trading one word for another word. It communicates the idea that certain actions must take place in order to establish a church, just like a wedding ceremony demands certain actions take place in order for a man and a woman to come together under the covenant of marriage.

First, covenanting demands that *a particular set of expectations* bind a group of Christians together, like biblical vows place a set of expectations on husband and wife. They are responsible to affirm one another's gospel professions. And they are responsible to oversee one another's discipleship.

Secondly, covenanting demands that a particular set of expectations bind *a particular group of Christians.* It makes clear who is meaningfully part of the church and who is not. We are a people "set apart" from the world.

How thin and meaningless the word "launch" seems by comparison! Covenant is a family word, a blood oath word. Launch is a rocketship word, or a widget factory word.

Finally, the word covenant communicates the idea that the church is a people, not an "event."

THE OLD MEETINGHOUSES

If you were to walk into the back of the old meetinghouses (as they called them) where churches gathered, you would sometimes find a beautiful document called a church covenant. It would lay out a way of life that the church had agreed to live by. At the bottom would be the signatures of the church's members.

I don't want to make too big a deal about what we call the beginning of a church. But I do think the word covenant will help to shepherd our people into a richer, deeper, and more biblical picture of what the life of the local church is and what it's not. Which suggests it just may be a practice worth recapturing.

Nathan Knight is the pastor of Restoration Church in Washington, D.C.

Personal Evangelism for the Church Planter and the Church Plant

by J. Mack Stiles

Most pastors I know start a church plant with a deep desire to do evangelism. In one sense, what else would you do? Hardly any new pastor sets out to start a church by "sheep stealing." They want a vibrant, cross-focused, Jesus-centered church that hums with gospel witness and is filled with excited new believers.

And they'll get right on it after they figure out how to set up a sound system in a high school gym, and puzzle out where the nursery is going to be held in the hotel, and deal with setting up the web page.

Though most pastors see evangelism as a key to spiritual health for the life of a believer and the life of the church, given the astonishing number of things that must be done for a new church plant—not to mention the internal sinful resistance to evangelism—it's easy to lose our fervor in evangelism. Evangelism, it seems, is always pushing the ball uphill.

> "Given the astonishing number of things that must be done for a new church plant, it's easy to lose our fervor in evangelism."

If evangelism is to be woven into the fabric of the life of a new church plant and its pastor, it takes some thought and planning.

Here are ten things I've learned that may help.

1. The time to start evangelism in your church plant is before you ever start the church.

If you've been so immersed in seminary or a support ministry such that you're separated from non-Christians, then you need to think about how you can treat evangelism as any other spiritual discipline.

Okay—let me tip my hand, if you've not been engaged in regular evangelism you probably shouldn't be starting a church. Regardless, regularly make attempts to share your faith now before you ever start to plant a church. If you wait until you get around to it, you won't ever get to it at all.

2. Teach, teach, teach.

Define the gospel: "The Message from God that leads us to salvation."

Define that message: "God, Man, Christ, Response," or "Creation, Fall, Redemption, Consummation."

Define evangelism: "Teaching (or preaching) the gospel with the aim to persuade."

Define biblical conversion, well, biblically. Check out Michael Lawrence's excellent book, *Conversion*, on the topic.

And when evangelism is demonstrated or commanded in the text of Scripture you're preaching through, make sure to highlight that for your congregation.

3. Go for low hanging fruit.

I once noticed a man who attended church occasionally with his wife. I bumped into him after the service and said, "Tim, I'm curious, where are you in your spiritual life?" "I'm not a believer," he told me. "I really just come to make Gina happy." We talked a bit more. I invited them over for lunch and we talked about spiritual life and the gospel.

Nothing much more happened, but Gina later told me that for all the years he was coming to church, nobody had ever asked him about his spiritual condition. Don't let that happen. Many people who show up in church are surprised when people talk more about sports than spiritual truth, and over time it convinces them they're doing okay. Instead, nail your fear of man to the cross and ask new people about their spiritual life.

The best place for pastors and timid evangelists to do evangelism is with the people who come to church. They're in church, after all!

4. Don't assume the gospel.

Assuming the gospel is the quickest route to kill a church in a couple of generations. Recently I was in Portland, Oregon, and I noticed the city was filled with empty church buildings.

But there was once a day when vibrant Christians sacrificed their money and time to build those buildings. What happened? They began assuming the gospel. An assumed gospel leads to a twisted gospel, which leads to a lost gospel. And when the gospel is lost, the life blood of the church is drained out.

Check every sermon with a question: "Could a non-Christian come to faith through what I preached today?"

Check the songs you sing. Are you communicating that people can be close to God regardless of the condition of their heart? We do that when we stir affections with a great tune but sing gospel-less words.

Make sure the truth of the gospel is in congregational prayers and Scripture readings; make sure it's clarified in the sacraments (do you fence the Table?). Have people give testimonies to the church before they're baptized, checking it over with them beforehand to make sure the gospel is clear.

When you do membership interviews, make sure when someone is fuzzy on the gospel that they're really believers. Let people know you love talking about the gospel and will happily make time in your schedule to do that. This selects out those who have genuine interest.

Talk about the gospel often with those who love it; more people than you know are listening in, especially children.

5. Lead in evangelism.

I suppose this is obvious, but you need to lead in evangelism. It's not enough just to preach the gospel, though that's of first priority. The congregation will know if you're sharing your faith personally. Of course you're so busy with Christians that it makes your job more difficult. Yes, you have a hard job. But tell your congregation of your desire to share your faith, get them to pray, and tell them of your successes and failures.

6. Make sure that everyone is on game.

You want the whole church to speak of Jesus—not just the pastor. This is why the church should regularly be asked about their evangelistic opportunities. And don't forget: they can help you. Tell your members that, if it would help them, you'd love to talk with their non-Christian friends.

Perhaps you'd find it useful to get my book *Evangelism: How the Whole Church Speaks of Jesus* on why a healthy church is the most important means of evangelism.

Champion evangelists in the congregation. Pray for them corporately and ask them how it's going. If the congregation knows this a priority to the leadership of the church, then they're more likely to practice it as a priority in their lives.

Of course, you want to talk your people to talk about successful evangelistic opportunities, but don't forget to share stories of failure. Ninety-nine percent of my evangelistic efforts don't go anywhere, but when that happens it's helpful just to know that we're in the battle.

7. Be practical, but not pragmatic or programmatic.

Just like you, your congregation needs help to share their faith. But don't set up a bunch of evangelistic programs. I often say that programs are to evangelism what sugar is to nutrition. Programs may make you feel like you've done evangelism when you haven't, just as eating sugar may make you feel like you've eaten when you haven't.

Having said that, do help your congregation get in the game with some practical helps. Here's an example: Covenant Hope Church in Dubai had everyone write out five non-Christian friends on a card and had people pray about sharing with the folks on that list. How simple and practical. They had them put it in their purse or wallet and they refer to it regularly. Have them think through the plan: an invitation for coffee, an email with an invite to church, etc. Help your congregation understand that if everyone is sharing their faith it will be much more effective than any church-wide evangelistic program, no matter how large that might be.

8. Be bold and clear when you share your faith.

I don't mean be offensive and abrasive when you share your faith. I just mean take more risks in evangelism. Be honest; let people know where you're coming from. This may sound a bit strange, but one of the great things about being up front about your desire to talk to people about the gospel is that if you're rebuffed, you've saved a lot of time for them and you.

9. Know the gospel, speak the gospel, and live the gospel.

Know how to say the message of the gospel in clear and unassuming language, and make sure members of the congregation know how to say the gospel in a minute or two in their own words, too.

I've noticed something over the years in my attempts to share my faith: if you don't regularly ponder on, pray about, apply, and speak the gospel, then it will become fuzzy and distant. I think it's the spiritual maxim that what you have will be taken away from you—or, to employ a cliché: use it or lose it.

Help the congregation know how to apply the gospel to their lives in areas of sin and repentance, forgiveness and holiness. Help them see how the gospel is not just what gets us saved, but a well in the center of life that we should draw from daily.

Church Matters

10. Use books, not tracts.

For giveaways and welcome gifts for visitors, prioritize brief and readable books rather than tracts. Books like the one I wrote called *The Truth About Lies*, or *What is the Gospel?* by Greg Gilbert.

Don't be chintzy. Give out books that explain the gospel and train your members to be willing to go over the books with the seekers who get them.

J. Mack Stiles is the director of Messenger Ministries Inc., a think tank working to develop healthy missions. He and his wife, Leeann, have traveled and lived many places before landing in Erbil, Iraq, in July 2017, including 15 years in Dubai, UAE. Up until recently, he was the pastor of Erbil International Baptist Church. Mack resides in Louisville and is a member of Third Avenue Baptist Church.

Planting Churches for Pleasure, Not for Profit

by Nathan Knight

I f you pay any attention to the land of church planting, you'll quickly begin to wonder if business mogul Jim Collins has taken control of its command center. Phrases like "customer-to-owner," "church launch," "preview services," and "entrepreneurial" have become ubiquitous, whereas those wonderfully powerful phrases we hear from Paul—"ambition to preach the gospel," "shepherd the flock of God among you," "preach the Word!"—seem to have been forgotten.

This is unfortunate because what's needed to plant a church isn't the wisdom of Jim Collins, but the gospel of Jesus Christ and the Word that testifies to that gospel. A cheap shot, I know, but listen—if we're going to enjoy the pleasure of God in planting a church, then we need to forget about the practices of men which promise to gather crowds quickly and instead mine the depths of God's Word in order to build a people intentionally.

Below I offer three principles we should all consider so that we might plant churches for the infinite pleasure of God's glory over and against our own profit.

Bible, Not Business

God's Word is sufficient, even for church planting. Whatever practices we need to give ourselves to are right there in the Bible, so long as we take the time to see them.

Discipleship, membership, preaching, discipline, elders, deacons, ordinances—all these things are spoken of plainly in the Bible. Each of them is a good gift from God that functions like a prong to fasten the church to the very same gospel it's called to proclaim and protect. In other words, things like membership and elders aren't just features we work into a plant after we've gathered a crowd; they're necessary ingredients that make up the compelling community that illustrates the character of God to a watching world.

The average church planting book gives little attention to describing and understanding what a church actually is. With good intentions, no doubt, these books often encourage church planters to prioritize profitability, such that "success" means getting as many people into the room as quickly as possible so they can attend your service. Usually, biblical markers for defining a church as a people—holy, set apart from the world—is at best a distant voice. Sometimes, it's not heard at all.

What is a church? Why does the church exist? What has God told us will mark his people? What should be

> "if we're going to enjoy the pleasure of God in planting a church, then we need to forget about the practices of men which promise to gather crowds quickly and instead mine the depths of God's Word."

taught? Who should lead? What should these leaders look like? What is success? The Bible has careful instructions on all of these things, which means it's more than sufficient to be our church planting guide.

Pastors Not Presidents

We may be familiar with Jesus's last words to his disciples, but what are the last words of that great church planter, the Apostle Paul? "Pay careful attention to yourselves and to all the flock, in which the Holy Spirit has made you overseers, to care for the church of God, which he obtained with his own blood" (Acts 20:28). Paul pleaded with these pastors to be shepherds who care, who love the flock that Jesus spilt his own blood to save.

Planters should not be entrepreneurs beginning a lemonade stand for Jesus. They should be pastors who gently handle the sheep of Christ and passionately push the glorious news of the gospel to places and people yet unnamed.

Visitors and church members should know we're not in it for a bigger platform. Instead, our lives should communicate our care for their souls. People can find magnetic and tantalizing personalities who are devoted to a specific good or service anywhere, but the church should offer something different. People are tired of being gamed for other people's profits. They want physicians who listen, honest car mechanics, politicians who get their hands dirty, and baristas who know their name. It's hard to find those kinds of leaders in the world, but people interested in the gospel should be able to find integrity in any leader of Christ's church.

Let's stop all these questions about being "entrepreneurial" and let's ask more questions about whether or not prospective planters love and care for their wives and their kids. Let's ask them about the last time they got a phone call late in the evening and they took it, gladly, because they wanted to serve those in trouble with the gospel. Let's ask planters if they'd be content with a little so that the Lord might entrust them with a lot.

Relationships, Not Rivals

Before several of us chose to plant a church in Washington, D.C. together, not only did we talk to denominational leaders, we also—and more importantly—talked to godly people who actually lived in D.C. and were working. We did this for a few reasons.

First, we wanted to respect those who were already here. Secondly, in light of that, we wanted to hear from them if there were any gaps in the city that we could fill with a healthy, gospel-preaching church. We didn't want to preach the gospel where Christ had "already been named" (Rom. 15:20). Our lives are short, and the Lord has entrusted a lot to us. So we made it a priority to go to an underserved place, no matter whether or not it was a known or popular city. In fact, we actually had a couple of other cities on our radar that we pulled away from because it seemed a lot of good work was going on there and it was going to be difficult to find a spot.

I see CVSs, Walgreens, and Rite Aides popping up everywhere—right on top of one another—in order to try and take the market share as rivals. Unfortunately, I sometimes notice the same thing happening among church planters.

Instead of building relationships, they listen only to their own camp, like a denominational leader who doesn't reside there but has "jurisdiction." Other church planters don't even ask questions about oversaturation because they assume every city is under-served and in need of their help.

But look at the Apostle Paul. One of his great joys was the fellowship he had with other churches. We miss out on that when we see others as rivals instead of family members to love, serve, and learn from.

Indeed, one of my greatest pleasures in church planting has been partnering together with a family of churches in the same city, "striving side by side for the faith of the gospel" (Phil. 1:27). We work together, not apart. The more we talk and listen to one another across denominational lines, the more the gospel fans out across the world, rather than pile up in one place.

Nathan Knight is the pastor of Restoration Church in Washington, D.C.

Four Encouragements for Preaching in a Church Planting Context

by Clint Darst

You've looked upon the crowds and observed they are indeed harassed and helpless, like sheep without a shepherd. As you've grown in grace, you've increasingly felt our Lord's compassion for the lost. You have obeyed his call to plead to the Lord of the harvest to send out more laborers.

And you've answered the call to go. Your church has affirmed your character, gifting, and readiness. They have helped you identify a strategic location, develop a core team, and raise funds to plant a new church. You've moved to the area, started evangelistic Bible studies, and practiced hospitality. The day fast approaches when you will covenant together as a new church and launch public services.

You have preaching experience, but this will be the first time you've labored in the pulpit week in and week out.

As you step into this laborious, weighty, joyful, and glorious work, I offer you four simple encouragements.

1. PREACH THE WORD

That first Sunday in the pulpit will be exhilarating. Church members from your sending church, friends, family, and hopefully visitors from the community will gather to celebrate the birth of this new church. You will be overwhelmed and grateful.

However, it's likely the following weeks will feel very different, as sending church members, friends, and family return to their churches, leaving you to gather in a less than ideal location with far fewer people. What will you do when you feel less momentum? Or when you look up from your manuscript to see far fewer people than you hoped?

Brother pastor, preach the Word (2 Tim. 4:2). Trust the Holy Spirit to move in power as you disciple the congregation through faithful expository preaching.

Perhaps begin with the Gospel of Mark or John and encourage the church toward evangelistic relationships by looking at the life of Jesus. Or maybe you planted in an area dominated by cultural Christianity but lacking in robust churches. Then consider starting with the book of Galatians in hopes of clarifying the gospel.

Either way, preach the Word. Don't succumb to the pressure of gathering a crowd with gimmicks, entertainment, or eloquence. Jesus promised to build his church. He promised that those who build their lives on his Word will withstand the storms of life. Your church needs the Word. The Spirit must breathe on the new work for it to grow; therefore, build the new work on the Word that the Spirit himself breathed.

2. PREACH THE CROSS

The Apostle Paul showed up to a dumpster fire of a church in Corinth that looked painfully like the pagan city it was in. It was overrun with sexual immorality, rampant divisions, obsessed with oratory celebrities, and swimming around in syncretistic doctrinal beliefs. What was Paul's strategy to help the struggling church?

He resolved to know nothing among them like he knew the cross of Christ (1 Cor. 2:2). Instead of competing with celebrity orators, he preached the folly of the cross while gladly revealing his own weakness, fear, and trembling (1 Cor. 2:1–5). His weaknesses, the Spirit's power, and the cross of Christ were the perfect ingredients for the Corinthians to place their faith in the power of God rather than in Paul himself.

Brother, every week preach the cross of Christ. Give your people the good news. Teach them the glories of the cross from every text. If you win them with the cross, you will win them to the cross. If you win them with intelligence, you win them to intelligence. If you win them with humor, you win them to humor. Hold out Christ and him crucified, buried, resurrected, ascended, and sure to return.

No matter if your first year is full of Sundays with hundreds or merely dozens, preach the cross. No matter if you're preaching from a beautiful pulpit in an old church building or behind a music stand in a middle school cafeteria that reeks of the previous Friday's square pizza and tater tots, give them Christ crucified.

And preach the cross with the passion of one who is banking their present and eternal joy on it. If your heart is enflamed with the glories of the cross, your passion will remain steady rather than ebbing and flowing with the size of the crowd. This will disciple your people to delight in Christ and, out of the overflow of that delight, to take the good news of the cross to those who are like sheep without a shepherd.

> "If your heart is enflamed with the glories of the cross, your passion will remain steady rather than ebbing and flowing with the size of the crowd."

3. PREACH WITH EVANGELISTIC COMPASSION

I've already assumed you know the scene in Matthew 9. Jesus went throughout all the towns and villages preaching, teaching, and healing. He declared the good news and demonstrated great compassion to all kinds of people in all kinds of places. And in this scene, the Lord of the harvest demonstrates that we must live with open eyes, broken hearts, calloused knees, and beautiful feet.

Jesus saw the crowds. He saw their sin and suffering. The disciples almost certainly observed him looking at the crowds and witnessed the compassionate grimace. His heart was broken for the lost crowds. Then he turned to the twelve with compassion in his eyes and commanded them to pray to the Lord of the harvest to send out laborers. The disciples needed to hit their knees and plead for laborers.

And almost immediately, he sent them out. They were the answer to their own prayers. They were the beautiful feet sent to preach the good news.

Pastor, it is especially crucial that your congregation learn evangelistic compassion from you. As you preach the Word and the cross, use illustrations and applications to help them see, feel, pray, and share the gospel with their lost friends and family members. In your preaching, make sure they *see* and *hear* what compassion *feels* like. Exhort them to pray because only God can grant new life. But also equip them to share the gospel with bold compassion because God uses beautiful feet to spread the good news.

As you preach, remember that they are learning where to look, what to feel, where to turn, and what to do. Shepherd the church to live with open eyes, broken hearts, calloused knees, and beautiful feet.

4. PREACH WITH CONTEXTUAL WISDOM

Preach the Word and the cross, not only with evangelistic compassion, but with contextual wisdom. Paul became all things to all people that he might save a few (1 Cor. 9:22). We must not be overly obsessed with culture, but it is foolish to ignore something Paul clearly considered.

Learn the city or town where God has called you. Know the history. Learn the dominant culture. Learn the minority cultures. Work hard to understand the beauty and brokenness of that specific place and those specific people. The better you exegete the people you are praying for your congregation to reach, the easier it will be to illustrate and apply the Scripture to those people.

Remember: you are not preaching to your sending church. The congregation gathered is not the same congregation you left. Nor are you preaching to your like-minded pastor friends in your network or to your seminary classmates. God has called you to shepherd and equip this little flock to be salt and light in a particular place, at a particular time, to a particular people.

No doubt, the most important thing about your preaching and even the church is that which it has in common with all other faithful preachers and churches. However, contextual and cultural ignorance—or (even worse) contextual and cultural arrogance—will certainly not help equip your members to live with open eyes, broken hearts, calloused knees, and beautiful feet. Know and love the people in the place God has called your young congregation to serve and bear witness to.

CONCLUSION

Brother pastor, as you step behind that sacred desk or wobbly music stand, preach the Word. Make sure the meaning of the text determines the main point of the sermon. Every week, preach the cross. Make sure the gospel is crystal clear every time.

And as you do, model evangelistic compassion and contextual wisdom so that the gospel is compelling and makes sense to those whom God has called you to dwell among. As you labor in this glorious task, may the Spirit equip the saints and bring the dead to life.

Clint Darst is the Lead Pastor of King's Cross Church in Greensboro, North Carolina.

Church Planting Is Rarely Rapid

by Matthew Spandler-Davison

Before Europe's Iron Curtain fell and Albania's brutal communist regime collapsed in the early 1990s, Albania was the North Korea of Europe. It showed all the devastating effects of a wicked dictator's reign. Among other things, the church had been forced underground in those years, and most clergy were imprisoned, exiled, or killed.

When Albania opened up, some of the first people to enter were Jesus-loving missionaries who moved into this dark and troubled land with a sense of gospel urgency. What followed was a wave of evangelistic activities, conversions, and rapid church planting.

However, like so much in Albania today, the church is a disappointing reflection of unmet expectations. Why are there still so few healthy churches in Albania? Why is it so hard to find faithful gospel-preaching Albanian pastors? How is it that after millions of dollars and scores of missionaries Albania remains a spiritually dark place with very few thriving, gospel-centered churches?

One of the reasons why there are so few healthy churches in Albania today is because those early rapid evangelistic and church planting activities were not effectively underpinned by theological precision and a biblical understanding of conversion and the church. The zeal for rapid multiplication ultimately killed the growth.

The Trouble with Rapid Multiplication Methodology

Turning to think about church planting methodologies generally, we have all seen the glossy missionary agency websites and well-edited video clips. We have read the tweets and been amazed by the Facebook posts that celebrate mass conversions, spontaneous baptisms, and rapid growth in church planting. Might I suggest that we look beyond the numbers and ask some probing questions. How do these people define "church"? What do they consider to be a genuine conversion? How are they assessing the character, competencies, and biblical conviction of the leaders they have identified? How are they providing theological training to this rapidly growing number of church leaders? How are they tracking the health (theological and otherwise) of these new churches?

Rapid church-planting movements often follow what are perceived to be moments of mass conversions accompanied by spontaneous baptisms. Leaders are quickly identified—men who show some personality and charisma and the ability to attract others to come around them. They are given a basic training in evangelistic techniques and granted the title of *church planter*. Such men then assume responsibility for a group of new believers which they call a *church*.

In much of Southeast Asia, Latin America, and parts of Sub-Saharan Africa, church-planting movements are gathering pace and reproducing at dizzying speeds. I have heard one leader of a Church Planting Movement use language like this: "If a new believer has a Bible and the Holy Spirit then he has all he needs to plant a church."

Paul's Example

The church planting movement began in first-century Jerusalem and spread throughout Judea and onto Europe. Yet, when we read the New Testament, it's clear that theological precision and a robust ecclesiology underpinned this momentum. The Apostle Paul, a learned and well-educated man, went through a period of training and preparation before he began his first missionary journey.

When he went from town to town, he would often stay a while to evangelize, disciple, and train leaders. There is no indication that churches were started spontaneously or reproduced rapidly. Rather, the general rhythm of church planting involved a period of training and assessment of new indigenous leaders. Paul himself warned the churches not to lay hands too quickly on men and not to appoint a new believer to leadership in the life of a local church. Rather, leaders were to be assessed over time.

Paul's church planting strategy had a high view of ecclesiology. He took time to make sure that churches were preaching the truth, exposing heresies, appointing qualified leaders, overseeing the members, caring for the widows and orphans, and administering the ordinances appropriately. He did the hard work of establishing strong, gospel-centered leaders in strong, gospel-centered churches.

Don't be like Peter in Galatians 2:11–14. Due to his fear and respect of leaders from his own culture, Peter broke table fellowship with the Gentiles over what he may have believed were divinely ordained (old covenant) legal issues. But with the coming of the new covenant and the passing of the division between Jew and Gentile (see Eph. 2:13), those differences now added up to nothing more than cultural and ethnic distinctions. As such, Peter was in effect requiring those who were ethnically different than him to assimilate to his ethnicity for the sake of fellowship. Paul responded to such requirements by remarking that Peter was "not acting in line with the truth of the gospel." The gospel doesn't allow anyone to insist that their cultural or ethnic norms function as the standard for discipleship.

Two Great Threats

I have come to believe there are two great threats to gospel work in the world's poor and unengaged communities today: the prosperity gospel and the encouragement toward rapid multiplication.

These two threats often appear together. Prosperity preachers chase spontaneous and rapid signs of God moving. Yet the prosperity gospel is graceless, crossless, and depends on man-centered preaching and methodologies. Theological wolves prey on the poor. They seduce hearers with the bait of a gospel that promises health and wealth rather than grace and Christ. Likewise, planters who pursue rapid multiplication through mass conversions and spontaneous baptisms want to see immediate and spontaneous signs of God moving. Yet their methods often produce poorly trained leaders and poorly defined churches. In other words, similar dynamics impel both prosperity preaching and rapid multiplication, and when people mix them together, total confusion follows about what it means to be a Christian and what it means to be a church.

In the New Testament, a church is a publicly identifiable gathering of believers who have covenanted together to worship Christ as a display of his glory to the nations. A rightly ordered assembly correctly observes the ordinances of baptism and the Lord's Supper as visible markers of the redeemed. It is a group of believers who follow the leadership of tested, trained, and affirmed pastors who preach the Word and shepherd the flock. Establishing such churches cannot be done quickly or easily.

While I want to rejoice at the apparent movement of God when I read those glossy missionary pamphlets celebrating mass conversions and rapid church planting, I also want to heed Paul's words of caution not to lay hands on men too quickly. I have met many so-called "church planters" who are preaching a false gospel. I have

Church Matters

> "While I want to rejoice at the apparent movement of God when I read those glossy missionary pamphlets celebrating mass conversions and rapid church planting, I also want to heed Paul's words of caution not to lay hands on men too quickly."

seen many so-called "churches" fail to be orderly or gospel-centered. I have witnessed mass spontaneous baptisms in places like Nepal and yet saw little evidence of conversion in the lives of those who were making a public profession of faith in Jesus. Our task is urgent. But an urgent task completed carelessly rarely produces good results. We must not pursue expansion at the expense of faithfulness. Instead, we should pursue church planting with the same sense of urgency *and* carefulness as the apostles directed the early church to do.

Training and Assessment

A church planting movement that is not underpinned by theological training, assessment, and ongoing support for an indigenous leadership rarely survives the test of time. In my role as Director for Church in Hard Places, I have had the privilege of meeting hundreds of pastors and planters serving in some of the most remote, poor, and unengaged places on earth.

Over the past few years, we have worked to develop the Church in Hard Places Apprenticeship. We have enrolled over 400 church leaders in a two-year, non-residential training from some of the poorest, most remote, and least engaged places on earth. This training is followed by an assessment process for indigenous church planters and pastors, which examines a man's competencies and biblical convictions in order to discern if he is qualified and competent to serve as a pastor or planter of a church.

Ours is not the only way to train and assess, but I pray that over the long term the result will be the reproduction of many healthy churches that will withstand the test of time.

Training Takes Time, But Trained Leaders Last a Long Time

It takes time to plant a church. It always has. That is as true in Southeast Asia as it is in Southeast Albania. We are now training close to twenty men from Albania, North Macedonia, and Kosovo, who are seeking to be equipped and supported as they plant healthy churches in the Albanian-speaking world. The rigorous work of being equipped to preach and teach the Bible, evangelize, and make disciples can be a challenge for some, but those who persevere will go on to plant and lead churches that effectively engage their communities. It is not rapid, but praise God, it has been fruitful.

> "It takes time to plant a church. It always has."

One thing that is consistently clear to me is this: the churches that thrive and survive in the hard places are led by well-trained men who have been tested and affirmed as biblically-qualified leaders. Training takes time, but trained leaders last a long time.

Matthew Spandler-Davison is a pastor of Redeemer Fellowship Church in Bardstown, KY, the Vice President of Acts 29 for Global Outreach, and the co-founder of 20schemes.

The Church Planter's Second Priority: Raising Up Leaders

by Mike McKinley

A bout three weeks into my work as the leader of a church plant/ revitalization, I was able to put words to something that had been bugging me. Our group of fifteen was made up of people who had come from the sending church as well as a few remaining folk from the congregation we were trying to revitalize. Some members of the group were happy and joyful servants; others were skeptical that it was going to "work" but were willing to give it a try; and still others were distrustful and unhappy.

Yet the nagging feeling I finally was able to put into words: as dedicated as some of these people were, no one in the church cared as much as my wife and I did.

That's not meant as a criticism of others. It's simply the reality of church planting. For a church planter, the work can be all-consuming. It combines your religion with your career and your livelihood. The stakes feel very high, and it's unrealistic to expect other people to be as invested as you in the church's viability. I know from my own experience and from talking to other church planters that this realization can heighten feelings of isolation and loneliness.

What I longed for in those early days were others to come alongside me and bear the burden of leadership, responsibility, and care. Now, eighteen years later, I haven't felt a sense of being alone in the work in some time. I remember taking a sabbatical at year twelve and realizing that in my absence the church's other elders, staff, and deacons had been leading the congregation quite effectively.

YOU NEED TO RAISE UP LEADERS

So, if you're a church planter, you need to focus on preaching the Word first and foremost, week in and week out. Without that, whatever you're planting, it won't be a church. But after that, you must give yourself to developing and cultivating other leaders. Doing so has an impact that reaches far beyond your own personal need to have others share the burden of caring for the church. Here are three other benefits of developing leaders in your church plant.

1. Developing leaders is important for the health of church members.

The most important way you'll help your church members grow is by preaching the Word of God faithfully week in and week out. But pastoral ministry also involves a lot of one-on-one investment in people's lives, and even the most diligent church planter will have limits on the number of

people for whom he can care. By developing other leaders who can teach, disciple, evangelize, counsel, and shepherd the flock, you raise up others who can care for the health of all the church members.

> "By developing other leaders who can teach, disciple, evangelize, counsel, and shepherd the flock, you raise up others who can care for the health of all the church members."

2. Developing leaders is important for the health of the congregation as a whole.

Having all of the leadership concentrated in one individual is certainly unhealthy for that person, but it's also unhealthy for a church. A plurality of leadership means a congregation isn't held hostage to decisions that have been made without considering the church planter's biases, weaknesses, and blind spots. When more people are involved in a church's leadership, it's less likely that individual members will become dependent on the gifts and personality of the church planter (who may, after all, not be with them forever) and more likely that they'll be built into the life of the church as a whole.

3. Developing leaders is important for mission.

I don't know about your experience of the space-time continuum, but I've found that I can only be in one place at any given time. That means there are many places I can't be present to proclaim the gospel and disciple believers. Assuming that the same holds true for you, then you're going to need to invest in other people who can go out to places where you are not.

Planting new churches locally and internationally requires leaders who can initiate and oversee the work. Those leaders must come from somewhere, and so you need to invest in developing them.

Church planters have a million things to do, many of which seem urgent. Investing your time in cultivating new leaders might seem like slow work that doesn't produce immediate and measurable results. But in the long run, it'll help strengthen and expand the scope of your ministry.

HOW TO DO IT

Here are three suggestions for how to find and develop new leaders for your congregation.

1. Develop leaders by sharing responsibility.

A lot of church planters are control freaks. I don't know if the nature of the work attracts those kinds of people (because it's easier to direct a church you start than one that you inherit from somebody else) or if it makes us those kinds of people (because so much seems beyond our control). But you'll never be able to raise up new leaders if you're not willing to let other people share in the responsibility of teaching,

making decisions, and caring for the flock.

Some object that it's dangerous to let unqualified people lead the church, and I agree. You shouldn't do that. Instead, find people who meet the relevant biblical qualifications (Titus 1:5–9, I Tim. 3:1–13) and give them a chance to lead, even if they do things a bit differently than you.

2. Discover leaders by looking around.

Sometimes, a person's abilities and gifts are obvious and right on the surface. But as I look at the leaders our church has helped to raise up, I'd say a good number of them were people I would not have immediately considered as having "leadership potential." That might be because of personality (maybe they're quiet, introverted, unassuming) or culture (I've learned that leadership sometimes looks different for people from different cultures). But I know I've been guilty of overlooking people who eventually became effective leaders. So how do you discover these people? Look around your congregation and ask questions like:

- Who is already bearing spiritual fruit in the life of the church?
- To whom do people go for help or counsel?
- Who is already doing the work of serving and caring for others without having been given an office or a title?

3. Develop leaders by training.

This is where the rubber meets the road. Once you're committed to raising up new leaders and you've identified potential candidates, you need to start actually training them. This will look any number of different ways[1]—from one-on-one meetings to large group classes—but you must begin to intentionally invest in helping to grow the character and competencies that the individual will need for the specific service they render to the body.

---

1. *For one example, you can find the curriculum for the first leadership training course that I did in our church in an appendix to my book* Church Planting is for Wimps.

Mike McKinley is an author and the pastor of Sterling Park Baptist Church in Sterling, Virginia.

How to Do Ministry When You Have No Money

by Brian Davis

How do you do ministry when you don't have any money? How do you serve the Lord as a church planter while broke? After thirty years of experience, I assure you I have expertise. But wisdom comes from Scripture:

Keep your life free from the love of money, and be content with what you have, for he has said, "I will never leave you nor forsake you." So we can confidently say, "The Lord is my helper; I will not fear; what can man do to me?" (Heb. 13:5–6)

The text teaches us four things about doing ministry without money.

Be Careful
Be Content
Be Creative
Be Confident

1. Be Careful ("Keep your life free from love of money...")

Pastors and church planters should watch their souls closely. Our ministries should be without covetousness, which Colossians 3 calls idolatry. The Bible pushes pastors in particular here, as an elder must not be a "lover of money" (1 Tim. 3:3).

Money is useful and has its benefits. It's good for churches to pay their pastor so as not to muzzle the ox (1 Tim. 5:18). But don't long for money or trust in it, or equate the size of your budget with the power of God. Money measures neither God's ability nor the value of our efforts. Jesus warns us plainly, "No one can serve two masters. . . You cannot serve God and money."

Also, just because you don't have money doesn't mean you don't love it. If you grumble in your lack, your heart posture may not be service for Jesus but an inordinate affection for money.

A good litmus test for church planters is this: Is your willingness to serve dependent on the pay? Remember Paul's parting words to the Ephesian elders:

"I coveted no one's silver or gold or apparel. You yourselves know that these hands ministered to my necessities and to those who were with me. In all things I have shown you that by working hard in this way we must help the weak and remember the words of the Lord Jesus, how he himself said, 'It is more blessed to give than to receive.'" (Acts 20:33–35)

2. Be Content ("...and be content with what you have...")

Living without covetousness means being content with what you have. "Be satisfied with the present," says another translation. We rest in the providence and provision of God, knowing this: "I will never leave you nor forsake you." Pastor, how do you deal with not having money? You should think on the fact that you have God!

Worry only has one remedy: a mindfulness of God. God encourages us to ask for what we don't have, but then we're free to trust whatever he gives or doesn't (Matt. 6; Phil. 4:5–7).

So, does your ministry need more funding? Are there currently unmet needs? Paul's own support letter gives us the secret to contentment:

I have learned in whatever situation I am to be content. I know how to be brought low, and I know how to abound. In any and every circumstance, I have learned the secret of facing plenty and hunger, abundance and need. I can do all things *through him* who strengthens me. (Phil. 4:11–13)

If we're known and loved by Jesus, our situation can never improve because our status will never change. He has pledged himself to us. And his Great Commission hangs not on our bank accounts but on the fact that he possesses all authority on heaven and on earth, and he is with us.

C. S. Lewis put it this way: "He who has God and everything else has no more than he who has God only."[1]

Church Matters

> "C. S. Lewis put it this way: 'He who has God and everything else has no more than he who has God only.'"

Hebrews tells us that Jesus is the Son of God, the appointed heir of all things. He is preeminent. He is rich in possessions and power. All things were made for him, and through him the world was created—things on heaven and things on earth. The universe is upheld by the word of his power! He's seated at the right hand of majesty on High—not a chair, but a throne: "Your throne, O God, is forever and ever."

It's this same ruling and reigning Lord who is with us even now.

God sometimes denies our requests now to prepare us for permanent joy in glory. If God gave us everything we wanted, then we'd trust our things more than him. Do you not pray most when you need most?

Pastors and planters, be mature in your thinking: "He who did not spare his own Son but gave him up for us all, how will he not also with him graciously give us all things?" If he hasn't given you something, his denial is a gift. He owns all, he knows what's best, and he loves you.

3. Be Creative

Spurgeon in his book *Lectures to My Students* has a section where he marvels at the abilities of some to accomplish exceptional good with very humble means. Spurgeon humorously labels ministers who are broke as workers with "slender apparatus." He writes, "Work away, then, poor brother, for you may succeed in doing great things in your ministry, and if so, your welcome of 'Well done, good and faithful servant,' will be all the more emphatic because you labored under serious difficulties."

So, rather than bemoaning what you can't do, enjoy what you can do.

To restate the question from the beginning: How do you do stuff when you don't have money? Brothers, you simply do what you can do.

And guess what? The most powerful and important things you can do are all *free*! Prayer is free! Studying Scripture is free! Sharing the gospel is free! Gathering for fellowship is free! Admonishing the idle, encouraging the weary and faint-hearted, and helping the weak is free!

> "The most powerful and important things you can do are all free!"

Sometimes, the blessing of God in denying us resources is him removing the very things our hearts are tempted to trust in. And is it not true that in our lack we often learn how much we still have?

Be as creative as the book of God permits you, and then go and battle in his name! Like King David, we don't go armed from the armory of the world—no, our stones from the brook are promises from the Word of God.

4. Be confident.

The Lord is our helper, and as Philippians tells us, "God will supply every need according to his riches in glory in Christ Jesus."

Who is it that is with us? Hebrews offers a massive view of God, and if we're to be comforted and confident it will require that our theology is equally robust.

Finally, we must never forget it is our Lord's wisdom that assigns one talent to some, two talents to some, and five talents to others. We should also note that our Lord is not unreasonable. Charles Spurgeon is not more sympathetic to our situation than the Sovereign Lord who assigned it to us. If he has limited your resources, then he will not enlarge his expectations. No, he is looking for those of us to whom he has given little, to be faithful over little.

---

1 C. S. Lewis, *The Weight of Glory* (Harper Collins, 2001), 34.

Brian Davis was born and mostly raised in Detroit. Before moving to Minnesota, he spent 15 years in Philly where he met and married his lovely wife, Sonia, and went on to have three beautiful children: Spurgeon, Sibbes and Noelle.

Church Planting Across Ethnic Lines

by Joel Kurz

Fifteen years ago, my wife and I (both of us white) moved into a neighborhood where we were an ethnic minority. We wanted to plant a church. Over the years, our idealism has been crushed; we've hit rock bottom, experienced a rebirth of vision, and have slowly made progress. God has been incredibly kind as he has formed a diverse church in our neighborhood. The immediate context is mostly African-American, yet we're three blocks from a historically white neighborhood. Our church is roughly half black, half white, with a very small percentage of Asian and Latino.

BIBLICAL BASIS

First and foremost: it's biblical and right to do cross-cultural ministry. God does burden individuals from one culture to share the gospel and invest in another cultural setting. God burdened my Korean-American friend, Dan, to plant a church in a historically poor white neighborhood. God burdened my African-American friend, Marty, who grew up in the inner-city, to plant a church in the suburbs. God called a man named Paul, who wanted to work among his own people, to leave and take the gospel to the Gentiles. When God burdens a preacher for a people group, a neighborhood, or a block, it's right for that preacher to go and become all things to all people so that he might save some.

Reflecting on his own gospel work, the Apostle Paul wrote:

> For though I am free from all, I have made myself a servant to all, that I might win more of them. To the Jews I became as a Jew, in order to win Jews. To those under the law I became as one under the law (though not being myself under the law) that I might win those under the law. To those outside the law I became as one outside the law (not being outside the law of God but under the law of Christ) that I might win those outside the law. To the weak I became weak, that I might win the weak. I have become all things to all people, that by all means I might save some. I do it all for the sake of the gospel, that I may share with them in its blessings. (1 Cor. 9:19–23)

But you ask: "Won't someone from the home context make for a better witness?"

Not necessarily. Don't misunderstand: God calls all people to work to reach their fellows, but the gospel is "the power of God for salvation to everyone who believes" (Rom. 1:16). Additionally, the Apostle writes, "When I came to you, I did not come with eloquence

> "God may place the most unlikely vessel into a neighborhood so the only explanation for fruit is God's supernatural work.'"

or human wisdom as I proclaimed to you the testimony about God. For I resolved to know nothing while I was with you except Jesus Christ and him crucified" (1 Cor. 2:1–2).

What if God called Dan to the historically white neighborhood, Marty to the suburban neighborhood, and myself to an African-American neighborhood so that "faith might not rest in the wisdom of men but in the power of God"? God may place the most unlikely vessel into a neighborhood so the only explanation for fruit is God's supernatural work. Man cannot do this; only God can.

MOTIVES

However, fueled by biblical support, it's possible to rush into cross-cultural work without examining our *extra-biblical* motives. During my first few years, I was often questioned: "Why do *you* think you should plant a church here?" This initially took me by surprise as I had a lot to learn. But over time I realized that the question was a good one because it came from a place that was intimately familiar with the history of white superiority.

If you're eager to do cross-cultural ministry, here are a few questions you should be willing to ask yourself:

1. Why am I here? Are you here because of guilt, because you think you can save the day, or because you implicitly think your way of doing life and church is superior?"

2. Am I willing to submit to someone of a different ethnicity? Do you have a mentor who's familiar with this context? If not, why not? Are you willing to find one? What might they say about your decision to plant a church in your intended location?

3. Is there a need for a new church? Are there other indigenous gospel works that you might consider joining? Should you submit to another pastor in this context? Are the other churches here actually unhealthy or are they merely operating from a different set of cultural values?

Essentially, you must ask yourself, "Have I moved to this context unaware of the racial, ethnic, or cultural history and dynamics of the country and the community?"

LAND MINES

With those words of encouragement and examination, please allow me also to point out a few potential land mines:

Land Mine #1: Trying to Be Someone You're Not

There's absolutely nothing worse than a white man who changes his dialect when talking to an African American. Marty tells me of his friend of twenty years who still tries to "talk jive" to him. "Becoming all things" doesn't mean you forget your ethnic background and attempt to become another ethnicity. That's just annoying; it's also condescending. Remember your background and recognize any tensions your presence may arouse.

Land Mine #2: Imposing Your Own Culture on Other Ethnicities

You *do* have a culture. Your preaching style, liturgy, and hymns—including the way you sing them—are culturally influenced. Your cultural background has shaped your discipleship and ministry preferences. Your values, politics, and the way you talk about these things, are peppered with certain cultural standards.

Don't be like Peter in Galatians 2:11–14. Due to his fear and respect of leaders from his own culture, Peter broke table fellowship with the Gentiles over what he may have believed were divinely ordained (old covenant) legal issues. But with the coming of the new covenant and the passing of the division between Jew and Gentile (see Eph. 2:13), those differences now added up to nothing more than cultural and ethnic distinctions. As such, Peter was in effect requiring those who were ethnically different than him to assimilate to his ethnicity for the sake of fellowship. Paul responded to such requirements by remarking that Peter was "not acting in line with the truth of the gospel." The gospel doesn't allow anyone to insist that their cultural or ethnic norms function as the standard for discipleship.

Land Mine #3: Despising Those Who Do Look Like You

An unexpected temptation for many who are working in a cross-cultural context is to subtly disdain members of one's own ethnicity when joining one's church. A Korean-American pastor desiring to plant a "non-Korean church" confessed that it took him a while to accept the fact that he still attracts other Korean-Americans to his church. People of your own hue will be attracted to your church because of you, and you must accept that happily. Don't make cross-cultural work an idol.

Land Mine #4: Drifting Toward Familiar Spaces

At the same time, there's another unexpected temptation, which is the draw toward familiarity. I've known cross-cultural ministers who have moved into inner city neighborhoods, never once shopping in their corner stores, hanging in their streets, or eating at their food spots. Instead, they socialize exclusively in hipster neighborhoods with coffee shops.

In short, it's all too easy to enter a particular community with the heart for a particular demographic, and then spend all of your time with people outside the context.

It's been said that the biggest missionary challenge is to *remain a missionary*

> "As you carefully move forward in humility and with wisdom, be encouraged that God often uses cross-cultural work for his own glory."

once on the field. You will be drawn to socialize, mingle, and connect with those who look like you and are from the same background as you. This is natural. And yet, in order to remain a missionary, you must fight against these natural tendencies and intentionally develop cross-cultural friendships. You must learn to appreciate the values, pleasures, rhythms, and routines of your new neighbors. Sacrifice comfort and learn a new culture. Become all things to all people so that, by God's grace, you might win some.

CONCLUSION

I'm glad you want to serve a context different than your home culture. This demonstrates that God has torn down walls of ethnic division in your own life. As you carefully move forward in humility and with wisdom, be encouraged that God often uses cross-cultural work for his own glory.

Joel Kurz is the lead pastor of The Garden Church in Baltimore, Maryland. You can find him on Twitter at @joelkurz.

International Churches as Strategic Gospel Multipliers

by Caleb Greggson

H ow do you envision the gospel spreading to new places, among peoples who have never heard of Jesus Christ? Odds are, you have a pretty definite, unarticulated idea of what that should look like. Do you picture canoes, malaria, and a lonely missionary setting foot into a virgin jungle? That is certainly one way. Another way for strategic gospel advancement is English-speaking churches in non-English speaking contexts—often called "international churches." International churches can serve as a foothold or base camp for further gospel witness.

Let me give four examples of what that can look like.

1. Expats need Jesus, and expats can show Jesus.

People who speak your language are sprinkled across most major cities around the globe. They are retirees, business people, and university students, and they are typically embedded in those cities with their own

> "more foreign Christians in my Middle Eastern city will be good for the indigenous church in this city because, just like the scattered church of Acts 7, faithful Christians proclaim the gospel wherever they are."

sets of relationships. Imagine if God allowed some of us to be a means of helping some of them be brought to faith and discipled. What might that do for the gospel's witness in each of those countries? If an international church teaches these expats to work as unto Christ, equips them to give an account for the hope they have, and disciples them to care about the spiritual well-being of their colleagues or fellow students, what might God do? Such work amounts to training missionaries already on the field.

I believe that more foreign Christians in my Middle Eastern city will be good for the indigenous church in this city because, just like the scattered church of Acts 7, faithful Christians proclaim the gospel wherever they are.

2. Intentional, normal Christians can join the work.

David Platt, when serving as president of the IMB, presented the notion of multiple pathways for non-career missionaries to get overseas. His excellent idea remains difficult for a single parachurch organization to implement on its own. It takes churches building a missions-centric heart to broaden the vision of ordinary Christians moving overseas to do mission in the ordinary practices of life. Multiple pathways provide different avenues to meet people. For instance, the retiree in our church meets different kinds of people than I do. So too do the business person and the college student. Having people live and exist in different capacities multiplies the kinds of people in our city who have more natural opportunities to show Christ to the community and engage in gospel conversations.

An international church is the missing piece in making that vision of multiple pathways viable. Churches in the States need good churches on the ground where they can send retirees and college students. While a house church made up of missionaries can certainly be a landing place, that church is a lot harder to see from across the ocean. An international church that meets in a more *traditional* meeting place, perhaps has a website and presence in the community, is easier to discover. It's also easier for a church in the U.S. to see such a church as a valid option for sending members.

A few years ago, an older businessman with several clients in our region moved from Florida to our city. He and his wife wanted to move where there are few believers so they could be a witness. Our church helped that desire become a reality.

3. Missionaries need pastoral care.

A friend who works for a large sending organization has observed that this current generation is the most mobilized generation for missions the church has ever seen, at least in terms of numbers of people who have moved overseas for the sake of the Great Commission. It's also the least effective generation for missions—not in terms of eternal kingdom impact (which we are in no position to measure), but in terms of workers' duration. These days, the majority of those commissioned are back in their home country within five years. And one of the most commonly stated reasons for their return? Insufficient pastoral care.

Most missionaries I meet are confused about their own need for a local church. Never mind the detrimental effect it has on those they disciple, their lack of a church also damages their own durability. The missiologists promoting rapid multiplication may object to how their strategy is being implemented, but the fact of the matter is, many young missionaries trained in those methods understand the strategy to require them to avoid participation in any church. Sadly, local believers learn from this example. They believe what they see in the missionary's life, not what the missionary says. Consequently, they learn to affirm the idea of a church, but to never submit to a specific one. We need to do better than this. One way is for missionaries to join international churches. In doing so, they model what they want others to do.

In other circumstances, the relationship between a missionary and the indigenous church is fraught with difficulties due to cultural differences, economic disparities, or local history. Add to that the challenge of language, and many missionaries find themselves with no meaningful church attachment—even in places where churches exist.

To help with this, many sending organizations have developed increasingly sophisticated member care infrastructure. Member care employees essentially function as itinerant pastors for missionaries. But rather than innovating a system of pastoral care outside the context of the local church, why not utilize a church to build up missionaries, as a church does for all Christians? We never graduate out of our need for a church. Perhaps church involvement would help flagging missionaries persevere.

For multiple reasons, an international church can provide missionaries with the kind of pastoral support that every Christian ordinarily needs. John Calvin perceptively wrote, "We see that God, who might perfect his people in a moment, chooses not to bring them to manhood in any other way than by the education of the church," a school we spend our whole lives studying in. Missionaries also need that school— not just at the initiation of their labor, but throughout it. Engaging in an international church may reduce the amount of time a missionary can invest among local believers, but it will also help them to endure—and perhaps increase the quality of their time discipling local believers.

4. Language differences among churches can provoke kingdom cooperation.

Meaningful church cooperation has always been a challenge. It is a messy, inefficient process. Ungodly competition often displaces godly cooperation simply because it's easier to do it yourself than to expend energy learning about other ministries.

Being a church that meets in English in a city where most people do not speak English, our elders have often felt the pressure to build strong relationships with other local churches. We need somewhere to send new converts who don't speak English but do speak the majority language. The "problem" of being an English-speaking congregation in a non-English-speaking city is a gift from God. It puts a pressure on us to invest in and pray for the health of indigenous congregations so we can know and trust them enough to entrust souls to their care.

Personally, I think the simple decision to encourage new Christians to join other local churches has done more to advance a mentality of kingdom cooperation among churches in our area than any sermon or conversation. Our members' care for Christians who have now joined other local churches has enabled local believers to see our members' interest in their churches no longer as the attention of a competitor, but what it is: Christian love.

CONCLUSION

International churches can work as strategic platforms for enhancing existing gospel work in a city. This happens through a variety of approaches to cooperation and encouraging more people to relocate to an international city to live ordinary lives for gospel purposes.

Caleb Greggsen pastors an English-speaking church in Central Asia.

Revitalization with an Eye Toward Church Planting

by Matt Capps

O ver thirty years ago, my church was planted by three other local churches. Back then, several faithful men and women saw a need to have a church on the corner where we now meet. They made sacrifices and committed to bring our church into existence. Church planting has always been part of our story.

Our church has matured and adjusted to meet the needs of our growing community. But our history has not been without difficulty. During the first three decades, the church went through several pastoral transitions, built several buildings, and saw people come and go. When I was called to serve as lead pastor in 2015, the church faced a $1.5 million debt and hadn't fully exited the shadow of the 2007–2008 financial crisis. Even more, the membership and giving numbers had declined for over a decade. When I preached in view of a call, I made it clear to the church that I wasn't "coming to fix everything but to point them to the One who could. I was coming to preach the good news of Jesus Christ, to lead and shepherd them as I believe the Bible exhorts pastors to do."

When I arrived, the church certainly wasn't on its deathbed, but needed intentional leadership and care. It fell somewhere on the revitalization scale. The good news: we had a strong core of faithful members who were ready to move forward and be strong in the mission of God. I had no flashy plan; my only desire was to faithfully shepherd the church and entrust the fruit to God.

As a former church plant and now established church, I believed one of the best ways to invigorate the church was to lead the members to invest in church planting efforts. If you are currently leading a church that has never planted or regularly supported church plants, this can feel like a daunting task. This is especially true if your church is a revitalization effort. You might think, "We have bigger priorities right now." And some of your people might ask, "Why invest in other churches when we have our own church to build and so many people to reach right around us?" The members might even counter, "We've never done this before!"

I understand the sentiments, I've heard the same things, but the effort is well worth it for several reasons.

WHY CONSIDER PLANTING?

1. Church planting is a biblical priority.

I assume we agree that the church is God's "Plan A" to reach people for Jesus Christ, and its purpose explicitly feeds into her structure (Matt. 28:18–20; Acts 2:42–47). More so, the pattern of gospel expansion in Acts demonstrates the priority of church planting.

During Paul's three missionary journeys, he planted at least fourteen churches. By the end of the second century, there were churches throughout the Roman Empire and beyond. It's important to note that the Apostles didn't do this alone: churches planted churches. The pattern for centuries to reach people with the gospel has been to plant gospel-centered churches.

If your people revere God's Word, and as pastor you faithfully exposit texts that demonstrate church planting, it will not be hard to convince them of these things. Now, knowing how to lead them is a matter of pastoral wisdom and prayer.

2. Once the church is convicted of the priority of church planting, it's important to expose them to the necessity of faithful churches in gospel-impoverished areas.

Networks like Pillar and entities like the North American Mission Board have the statistics and information you need to educate your people. In fact, the more you talk about church planting, you might find that your people have connections to certain cities or find that God has given them a heart for a certain place which needs a faithful church. As part of this education process, invite your people to get to know church planters or participate in short trips to aid planters in evangelistic efforts or service projects. Once you educate the congregation on needs and develop an affinity towards a certain location or plant, it's natural to develop a partnership or to send some of your people to join those efforts.

Church Matters

3. To develop an eye toward church planting, you must lead your people to put their money where their heart is.

Financial support will always be one of church planting's greatest needs. The end goal is always for the new local congregation to become financially self-sustaining in time. In the early years, it is safe to assume that most, if not all of a church plant's financial support, will come from other churches or individuals. In the New Testament letters, we see glimpses of partnerships that were mutually transformational for church plants and support churches (Phil. 4:16; 2 Cor. 11:8-9).

One way to revitalize and invigorate an existing church is to lead them to invest in God's work above and beyond themselves. In most cases, regularly giving to church plants also encourages greater generosity within the existing church. It's important then to teach your people to hold their resources with an open hand and be ready to willingly give toward God's work outside their own walls.

4. Pray that God would equip your existing church to build to the place where a church planting team can be sent out.

Again, if churches plant churches, and if church planting is truly essential to the mission of God, then every church should pray and work towards being a sending church or partnering with sending churches.

One of the ways we have begun to position ourselves to do this is by starting a Ministry Training Center to attract interns as potential church planters. The idea is once they have served among us, we want them to recruit other members from our church to go with them. Once they are ready, our desire is to commission and release them to plant a new church and trust that God will fill whatever voids are left.

> "if church planting is truly essential to the mission of God, then every church should pray and work towards being a sending church or partnering with sending churches."

TAKING THE BIG STEP

Over the past eight years, this is how we have led our church to be involved in church planting. It's taken patience and persistence. Our financial stability strengthened as we increased in generosity. In fact, we paid off our debt in four years. Our membership has strengthened even as we've increased our attention on the needs of church plants outside our four walls. We're currently asking God to provide so that we can accomplish sending out our own church plant.

In this process, I have seen God enlarge our people's vision for his work in the world. I have seen our people give generously to church plants in need while faithfully supporting church planting in our annual budget. In many ways, I believe our obedience in this area has been a contributing factor to our health and maturation.

If you are currently in the midst of a revitalization, don't necessarily neglect church planting. Prayerfully seek to be faithful with whatever opportunities come your way. After all, in the kingdom of God we can accomplish more together than apart. This is why church planting isn't just a ministry for individual church planters—it's a ministry

"If you are currently in the midst of a revitalization, don't necessarily neglect church planting."

for the whole (universal) church. And partnership is not only beneficial for the plant, but for the established church as well.

Matt Capps is the Senior Pastor of Fairview Baptist Church in Apex, NC.

Church Planters, Don't Wait to Put Your Documents in Place!

by Joel Kurz

W e waited three years to put our church documents in order, and we suffered for it.

We had a statement of faith—we needed one for funding—but we didn't know how to use it. No one ever encouraged us to adopt (and take seriously) a constitution or church covenant. Even if they did, I wouldn't have listened.

Church documents seemed outdated and rigid. I wanted to reach the people who the "other churches" weren't reaching. I wanted the people who didn't like the church, the people who were looking for something different.

Three years in, we put documents in place—and it was painful.

By that time, we'd attracted a group of people, many of whom disdained the local church. We knew that we were against legalistic and rigid churches, but we did not know what kind of church we wanted to become. Everything seemed up for discussion and debate, including the inerrancy of Scripture and substitutionary atonement. With no concept or ability to exercise church discipline, sin went unchecked. Challenges didn't work because everyone appealed to personal taste and would offer to "agree to disagree."

After three years of this, it was pretty clear that we were sinking. If Jesus's prayer was for unity in the church, his request didn't seem to be answered in ours.

Finally, we put a few documents in place. Our statement of faith took a prominent role in establishing what the church believed the Bible teaches. After many conversations and much research, we established a church constitution. We found a time-tested church covenant that simply outlined what the Bible requires of all believers.

And in the months to follow many people left, some angry, others frustrated.

So . . .

Church planters, don't wait three years to put some documents in place!

THE CHURCH IS A COUNTER-CULTURAL INSTITUTION

A restaurant may be organized a hundred different ways. The best of human wisdom can organize an excellent non-profit. But only Jesus can organize the local church. The Bible is where we find its organizing principles, and let me tell you: the church is *quite* the counter-cultural institution!

As you read the responsibilities that church members have for one another in passages like 1 Corinthians 5, or the leadership qualifications in 1 Timothy 3, you immediately get a profound sense that "flying by the seat of the pants" (as my mother would say) while organizing a new church just won't do. Without clear biblical guidelines, the new church plant may very well blend with pop-culture, but it will grow in unhealthy ways.

Theological Fuzziness

Drawing theological lines seems counterintuitive in our postmodern era. However, church plants don't naturally drift into orthodoxy. Not establishing doctrinal lines from the beginning causes the church to drift away from unity, integrity, and God's revealed truth. As a result, the budding church will likely be distracted by endless debates on core issues such as inerrancy and substitutionary atonement instead of engaging in what the planter *really* wants to engage in: mission!

Ecclesiological Squishiness

Who leads the church? Who is a church member and what's required of them? Who can serve in the church? Before our church was organized, the diversity of answers we received to questions like these questions was tremendous. Biblical church polity across the board is counter-cultural in society. Male eldership, congregational authority (for us Baptists), a baptized and regenerate church membership—these aren't ideas that we just come up with on our own. A church with no guiding principles on church government will likely guide itself right out of biblical faithfulness.

Moral Ambiguity

What is required of a church member, and who determines this? A church plant without documents sets up their new flock for confusion. Can a cohabiting couple become members? Can a man living in clear, unrepentant sin serve in a public ministry? How do we handle a sister rebelling against Jesus?

Without clear biblical documents, church plants will drift toward legalism or licentiousness. Legalistically, they may place upon their members spiritual requirements that Jesus himself does not place upon them. Alternatively, their members may be given over to sin, having embraced an unchecked licentious lifestyle.

Because sinful people are called to plant and organize local churches, we need guiding principles that transcend human wisdom. We need biblical guidelines from the start.

THIS IS WHAT A CHURCH IS, AND WHO WE NEED TO BECOME

As a pastor, I often have the opportunity to counsel engaged couples. As part of our pre-marital counseling, I always explain in detail the expectations and requirements of marriage. Can you imagine someone getting married, and discovering the expectations and requirements of marriage three years later?

Lack of forethought and clarity as to *who* the church is and *what* the church does will lead to endless divisions. Responding to those divisions with documents (three years later) will

feel reactionary and people will leave. Starting off with the documents will say from the get-go: "This is what the church is, and this is what we need to become."

Having documents at the beginning says: "We're a people of the Book."

Sometimes people ask, "Isn't the Bible enough?"

Well, in a sinless world, perhaps, we would all agree on what the Bible teaches. But in a fallen world, various interpretations abound. Biblically saturated documents communicate that a church plant's vision is to be "built upon the foundation of the Apostles and Prophets" (Eph. 2:20).

By finally establishing documents, we were able to speak clearly to the people that God had given us, "This is what we believe the Bible says, and it's on this foundation that we stand. We not only recognize the need for biblical church leadership, but we spell it out. Ultimately, our documents detail and cast a vision for who we as a church will become. We not only admit that the Bible calls for pastoral integrity, but we formally place ourselves under the accountability of the church. These documents will provide you, church, protection from renegade, spineless, and authoritarian church planters. We not only discuss what membership looks like, but we detail what God requires of the Christian—and what we, as a church, expect. These documents provide instant help when dealing with unrepentant sin and church discipline cases. They provide a vision of discipleship of each of our church plant team members, as well as new converts. We not only preach Galatians 1:6

(that we must not turn to another gospel), but we use these tools to articulate what that one true gospel is. These documents serve to protect the church from false teachers and wolves."

TOOLS FOR DISCIPLESHIP

The Bible instructs churches to organize themselves in a way that flies in the face of current culture and fallen wisdom. Because of this, church plants need documents.

"We as a church grew significantly in spiritual health once we voted those (documents) in," said one member who's been with us since the

> "The Bible instructs churches to organize themselves in a way that flies in the face of current culture and fallen wisdom."

beginning. It changed our church, and it changed our members. While some left, others responded positively, embraced the biblical vision, submitted themselves to the local church, and grew. Church planting is about making disciples, and documents are useful disciple-making tools.

Joel Kurz is the lead pastor of The Garden Church in Baltimore, Maryland. You can find him on Twitter at @joelkurz.

Church Planters, Make Sure Your People Know You Love Them

by Steve Jennings

I once asked a long-time pastor: "What's one piece of advice you would give a first-time pastor preparing to plant a church?"

His answer? "Before you do anything else, make sure your people know you love them."

WHAT LOVE IS NOT AND IS

Sometimes it helps to know what loving our people *is not* before we know what *it is*. It's not always telling them what they want to hear, or being a people pleaser, or even trying to get them to love you in return, whatever it takes.

In fact, loving our people isn't about us at all. Rather, to love your people means to show them how dear they are to you by gently and sacrificially giving of yourself to feed them with the nourishment of the gospel for both their eternal good and God's glory. To follow Paul's analogy from 1 Thessalonians 2, loving them means seeking their good at your expense, their flourishing above your recognition—like a mother. You love them because they are dear to you, having been placed into your care by God.

AIMING FOR LOVE

So, from day one, I endeavored to make that my aim. More often than not, I failed miserably. But by God's grace, I've also seen some fruit.

In the earliest days of our church plant, striving to make sure I loved my people and that they knew it meant at least four things:

1. Disagreement with Unity

My city is diverse, and there aren't a lot of options around for a church, which means a wide variety of people come to us. There have been times when people have come and disagreed on a variety of practical and/or tertiary doctrinal points, but they've stayed and listened because they sensed that they were loved.

> "to love your people means to show them how dear they are to you by gently and sacrificially giving of yourself to feed them with the nourishment of the gospel for both their eternal good and God's glory."

2. Reception of Hard Words

When people are confident that they're loved, they're more prepared to receive rebuke. On the other side, I've also experienced what happens when I've not laid the foundation of love and then confronted sin. The difference is staggering.

3. Cultural Barriers Transcended

My church is very culturally diverse. Caring for people through simple, consistent sacrifice means that we can eventually overcome many cultural barriers, such as different customs of hospitality or expectations for liturgical structures. We've had people from different countries who struggled with our music or preaching style, for instance, but they stayed because they sensed the shepherds genuinely cared for them.

4. Understanding for Pastoral Imperfections

Laying the foundation of love has meant an abundance of patience with my own immaturity and failings as a pastor. And we pastors, as fellow sinners, need lots of that. Our people need a context for understanding our shortcomings. They need to know we're imperfect and trust in Christ as our only hope—just like we exhort them to do.

HOW TO PURSUE LOVE

Again, before we can show our people we love them, we must actually love them. And if we're honest, this can be hard, and it's not always something that comes automatically.

So how do we pursue it? A few ideas:

1. Daily pray for your heart to be filled with love for them and then pray for specific people.

Make it a habit of praying each day, "Lord, help me to love you, to love my family, and to love your people more." Have a practice of praying for each one by name, such as praying through your membership directory.

2. Soak in the gospel.

1 John and Ephesians 5 show us the source of our love for our people: a heart-deep knowledge of the love of God expressed in the death of Christ for us. The fountain of our love for our people must be the gospel. Otherwise, we will be fickle and our love will be aimed at the wrong ends.

3. Spend time with them.

Love is cultivated through fellowship. To move from love as an idea to love as a reality, there must be a cultivated relationship.

COMMUNICATING LOVE

Finally, how do we communicate love to our people? How do we, before anything else, make sure they know we love them?

1. Show hospitality by spending time with them.

Like Paul and the Thessalonians, it must be clear that we don't just preach to them, but that we're sharing our lives with them as well.

Hospitality both grows and shows our love for them. It's important to set up a schedule of pastoral visits and ask questions that show they're important. It's in this context that the little things matter—remembering birthdays, being aware of burdens and illnesses, showing an appreciation for things they enjoy—much like a mother would for her child.

During these times, share with them truth from Scripture and gentle encouragements and admonitions that relate to their current affairs in life, or just listen to them talk. Take note of what's burdening them and what they're rejoicing in and remember it as you pray for them.

2. Listen well to complaints and criticism.

When those first difficult words come at you—and they will—listen to them with a calmness that's rooted in your position in Christ. Don't immediately respond to criticism; instead, hear people out and be very, very quick to admit your own faults. Realize that God is using them for your sanctification too.

Every criticism I've ever heard has offered something I needed to hear. It's in these difficult moments that your love for them can become the most visible and transformative.

3. Pray with them.

Pastoral ministry can be scary. There are many times that we care but we just don't know what to say. Thankfully, no matter the situation, we can always pray. Earnest prayer with your people is perhaps the most powerful tool for expressing your love while at the same time pointing them to the One who loves them perfectly.

> "he way we express our love for our Savior is through our love for his people."

4. Preach like you love them.

You'll exhibit your love for your people through careful, relationship-informed, gospel-soaked preaching. If you show them outside the pulpit that you care for them, then your expository ministry will flourish in the context of relationships. And that's powerful. When they hear and see you preach, do they see a man who's engaged in a labor of love? They should.

CONCLUSION

Looking at Jesus's words to Peter post-resurrection, we're reminded that the way we express our love for our Savior is through our love for his people. So, when laying the foundation for a new plant or revitalization, there are few pieces of advice better than this: before you do anything else, make sure your people know that you love them.

Like Peter, who had recently experienced the love of his Master, let the love of Christ control us to such a degree that we view the people in our charge differently. Let us love them as members of the body of the Savior we love and that by loving him, we love them.

Steve Jennings is the pastor of Immanuel Church of Fujairah in the United Arab Emirates.

Church Planting in the Same Building

by Matthew Spandler-Davison

O n Sunday morning, as I sit in my office to prepare for worship, I can hear the muffled sounds of singing and preaching coming from the main hall in our building. Pre-school aged children are playing in the classroom next to my office. The aroma of brewed coffee comes from the kitchen. Communion cups have already been prepared.

And yet . . . no one from our church has arrived. Instead, at 8:30 a.m. on a Sunday morning, members of Grace Fellowship Church in Bardstown, Kentucky, have gathered for their weekly worship gathering. It's a church we planted, and it's a church with whom we're delighted to share our property.

We planted a church in our own building.

THE STORY

In 2012, the elders of Bardstown Christian Fellowship (my church) presented to our members a proposal for what we termed "On-Site Church

> "We're convinced our community in central Kentucky doesn't need more church buildings, but more healthy churches."

Planting." The early years of Bardstown Christian Fellowship, a church planted south of Louisville, were difficult. Evangelism proved an uphill struggle in an area where only one in ten people are active in church, and half are Roman Catholic. The church experienced slow but steady growth over the first decade. In 2011, the elders recognized we'd soon outgrow our meeting space. We had little enthusiasm for spending more money on a bigger building. Neither did we have any desire to start a second worship service. So, committed to reaching the lost through church planting, the elders were led to start a second church.

What we did next is unusual. We planted this second church in the same building. Two churches, one location. One meets at 8:30, the other at 11:00.

We launched Grace Fellowship Church in August 2012. We commissioned three of our elders and a number of families to start this new work. We started the BCF Network, which owns the property and its furnishings. The member churches have equal access to the property. As churches, we've pooled our resources so that we hold everything in common. We jointly fund a church administrator, and we share the expenses of the facilities. This is our long-term strategy, to make the facility available as a public space in which like-minded churches can gather for worship and partner together to reach our city and the nations.

Grace Fellowship (the newer church) has already celebrated a number of baptisms and is connecting with people we never reached. We're convinced our community in central Kentucky doesn't need more church buildings, but more healthy churches. Churches in small-town America already own enough properties; they just need to be more strategic in how we're using them.

THE RATIONALE: WHAT IS A CHURCH

Many pastors I've shared this story with have raised their hands up in complete confusion. They ask, "Why would you do that? "In order to best understand the rationale for the creation of a property-sharing network of churches, it's first necessary to be clear about what a church is. Most Christians would acknowledge a church is not a building but the people—and yet, when we strip away a building from a church, we begin to question the legitimacy or viability of that church.

> "Churches in small-town America already own enough properties; they just need to be more strategic in how we're using them."

A growing church has options to consider when dealing with practical issues related to space and organization. Many would consider starting multiple services or campuses. However, to do so distorts the very nature of the church.

Jesus uses the word *ekklesia* when referring to the church in Matthew 18:17. When a brother sins against another brother and does not repent, then a decision is deferred to the gathered congregation of believers, the *ekklesia*, to remove him from that local and visible body of believers. In using the term, Jesus indicates that the act of assembling together as one group is integral to the authority and identity of a particular church. In Matthew 18, Christ grants authority to the identifiable assembly of Christians to determine who is, or is not, a member of the church. Multiple assemblies, therefore, suggest multiple churches.

Jonathan Leeman puts it this way,

What shall we say constitutes a local church on earth? The answer which the Bible gives, I think, is simple and straightforward: a local church is constituted by a group of Christians gathering together bearing Christ's own authority in the gospel to exercise the power of the keys of binding and loosing through the ordinances.

A church then, as Leeman correctly points out, is a gathering of Christians that exercises the authority given to it in order to fulfill the mission it has received so that it can be a display of Christ to the watching world. A group that doesn't regularly gather at one time and in one place is therefore not a church as understood by the use of the term *ekklesia* in Matthew 18.

"I simply want to offer an alternative to a costly building campaign or tying up resources in more bricks and mortar. That alternative is establishing a network of churches that partner together to share property and resources, and support each other in the work of the ministry."

This understanding of the church as being a visible assembly of believers that worship together is key to understanding the rationale for Bardstown Christian Fellowship and our choice to develop a network of churches rather than starting multiple services or sites.

YOU COULD DO IT, TOO

Many growing churches are in towns and cities where members drive by many other church buildings in order to get to their own church service. In other words, just because a church meets in a particular neighborhood doesn't mean it will only effectively reach that particular neighborhood. Furthermore, sending a group of believers to a separate location necessitates duplicating resources and investing funds in new accommodations and equipment, funds that could perhaps be better spent on missions and ministry.

Acknowledging this, a growing church might consider a new gathering place or building a larger building. This is a perfectly reasonable response to growth—though it's often a costly one. A church gathering in a city with extremely high property values, or a church meeting in a nation where it's difficult to own property, will find this option increasingly out of reach.

I simply want to offer an alternative to a costly building campaign or tying up resources in more bricks and mortar. That alternative is establishing a network of churches that partner together to share property and resources, and support each other in the work of the ministry.

The Bardstown Christian Fellowship of Churches is an example of just that: a network of like-minded churches that share the same property, jointly fund administrative staff, and work together to make disciples of all nations.

Matthew Spandler-Davison is a pastor of Redeemer Fellowship Church in Bardstown, KY, the Vice President of Acts 29 for Global Outreach, and the co-founder of 20schemes.

Church Planting by Peaceable Division

by Colin Clark

I n September our church did something crazy: we planted a church on
the other side of our city.

Or maybe that doesn't sound crazy. But hold on. We planted by literally *dividing our church in half,* and we did this as a relatively small and
young church.

We didn't grow to 800 and send out thirty. Our three-year-old church
had 84 members before the plant, and 45 after. Our financial giving was
reduced by more than fifty percent. Pre-plant, there were four families in
my apartment complex; post-plant, only my family remained.

That very same week, there was an article here at 9Marks called
"Church Planting by Peaceable Division." To call it timely would be a
massive understatement. The article highlights the historical prevalence
of churches intentionally and amicably splitting for the proclamation of
the gospel and the glory of God.

This is what we did, and I offer six lessons we learned from the process.

1. **God leads even young, small churches to plant; it's not a mission merely for large, established churches.**

Even as we were walking through our decision, there was something in me that fought back against it. Why? Well, our church hadn't had time to "come into our own" yet. We could have used more elders and more leaders, not to mention people in general! Our budget could have been healthier. We could have taught on church planting a bit more.

All such hesitancies should be weighed seriously. If you are going to ask your congregation to do something painful, they need to understand the *why*. It's good stewardship to consider budgets, and it's wise to consider leadership capacity. But logistics can become too important and hinder churches from obedience.

At our church, we were quickly approaching size constraints. We looked at a map of our city and realized nearly half of our folks were traveling to the northeast part of the city, where we meet, from the southwest. Some even drove three hours round-trip. So we pushed ahead.

Maybe God is calling your church to plant before you're ready, too?

But why not just secure a bigger facility or start a satellite campus in the southeast? That leads to a second lesson.

2. **The heat of planting tests and reveals a church's ecclesiological priorities.**

"To plant or not to plant" will always drive us to ask why we exist as a church. Is our ultimate goal comfortable community or missional community? How important is it that our church members live in proximity to the church and other church members? Do we more highly value having our act together in one place before reaching out to another? How highly do we value financial sustainability at the "mother church" before sending healthy members out from us? Do we desire to grow one big church in one neighborhood or to have two smaller churches in two neighborhoods? Do we think the local church is an assembly, or do we think it is viable to have multiple locations and call them one church? What about "protecting our DNA"—popular nomenclature these days—and our preaching ministry? Do we care about that? And if so, how much?

I'm not trying to tell you how each of those questions should be answered. I'm just saying this is a huge lesson in church planting—and you should be ready for it. Your priorities will be put on an operating table for everyone to poke and examine. You'll have to answer questions you didn't even know were questions and to question things you thought you'd already answered!

3. Church planting reinforces gospel motivation.

This lesson wasn't really on my radar, honestly, but it was a pleasant surprise. Our plant reinforced gospel motivation—and not just in the obvious ways about how we want more people to hear God's Word and be exposed to gospel witness.

What I mean is it made me realize that the gospel must be the driving force behind each young man I disciple, each person I evangelize, each couple I counsel on our living room couch. Once you decide to be a church-planting church—and especially if you plant by peaceable division—it's far too easy to be far too "strategic" with your time. We all have boundaries and filters, to be sure, but should I keep counseling this couple when I know they'll be heading to the church plant in three months? Should I keep building into this potential elder when he'll likely be an elder in the other church and not mine?

Of course I should! And I should because the point of ministry isn't building my own kingdom; it's building God's. I'd hope the gospel would motivate me regardless, but the process of planting reinforced it for me.

4. Church planting by peaceable division *presents* unique *pastoral challenges.*

Let me list a few:

- Your elders have to lead courageously like never before. Emotionally, nobody wants to plant,

and it will almost certainly stall out unless you have leaders out front with the standard.

- Your elders need to be on the same page about how to counsel members. There will be a ton of questions: *Should I stay or go? What if one church is closer to my home but the other is closer to my work? When do I have to make a decision? What is the process if I want to go? What things should I consider if I'm equidistant to both churches? What if I'm closer to one church but my mom's group will end up at the other church? Do I just get to pick or are the elders making a recommendation about where I should go?* The questions will come. Be ready.

- If you're planting by peaceable division, both churches will feel like church plants for a while. Help members think about the needs at both churches as they're making their decisions.

- Get on the same page with other elders and communicate well. Will any elders be "recruiting" for either church? Do we want this to happen at one church but not the other? Who are some of the key leaders each pastor is hoping to have on their team once the dust settles? Over-communicate on the front end and talk through as much as you can—it will serve you well.

- One of the biggest challenges for me was that I processed the reality of the plant far earlier than everyone else. This caused me to be less empathetic once the plant happened. I had mentally moved on while many of our members were dealing with it afresh. As a result, I'm not sure I was in a good place to shepherd them as well as I could have.

These are just a few of the unique challenges and opportunities. You'll have your own; be reflective and patient.

5. Church planting *is an opportunity for Satan.*

This one is obvious, but church planting accompanies unique temptation for division, disputes, and hurt feelings. Be on the lookout for opportunities Satan may use to drive relational wedges that cause disunity. We should always give the benefit of the doubt to our friends, assume godly motives among godly leaders, and be wary of the sin in our own hearts.

Any time there's a plant, Satan will tempt Church A to keep a watchful eye on Church B. This is good insofar as the "mother church" wants to make sure the plant is growing in the joy of the Lord and remains free from false gospels. Yet churches must guard against competitiveness or being suspicious anytime the other church does something new or different.

While we're certainly not perfect, we've worked to remain on the "same team." Both churches frequently pray for each other publicly during the morning and evening gatherings. We share pulpits with each other. If we bring a guest speaker in town, we try to share. We invite each other to events, conferences,

and some retreats. We formed an association (our two churches plus others) to band together for pastoral training, church planting, and missions. Be on the lookout for ways Satan will use this for *his* good and fight the good fight.

6. Church planting *is really hard but really worth it.*

I'll put it all together in one final lesson: church planting by peaceable division was really, really hard, but also really, really worth it. The biggest struggles for us involved emotional difficulties: friendships complicated, healthy community shaken up. The smaller your church and the deeper your community, the bigger this struggle will be.

And to that, we say, "Praise God!" What a great problem to have! This is true, but it also doesn't make the struggle any less real or difficult.

On top of that came the difficulties of not having enough elders, deacons, and money. Our church was left with less experienced preachers; we also lost a majority of the large families. I could go on because the list of challenges isn't short.

But for all the burdens, we experienced far more blessings. On any given Sunday, our churches have attendees from six of the seven continents, and they'll all hear the gospel. Our church in the northeast has had more room for more people to come in and hear God's Word proclaimed, and the plant in the southwest has been able to provide a healthy church for many who hadn't heard of our church or

> "church planting by
> peaceable division
> was really, really hard,
> but also really, really
> worth it."

who had but didn't want to make the hour-plus trek across the city. We've also been able to start an association that seeks to strengthen even more local churches.

On a personal level, the whole experience of church planting strengthened my faith. I had to trust God like never before and take my hands off situations that, in my flesh, I so greatly wanted to manipulate. God met me—and all of us—in the midst of any confusion, and truly gave us peace that surpasses understanding.

May it be so for you as well. Pray for us—that we'd be willing, joyful, and expectant should God entrust us with such an opportunity again.

Colin Clark is an international pastor in East Asia. You can reach him via info@www.9marks.org.

Section Four

Church Planting in Hindsight

Church Planting Roundtable: Counting the Cost

by Will Forrest, John Joseph, Zhang San,
Joshua Chatman, Caleb Greggsen, Trell Ross

C hurch planting, in one sense, is just like any other pastoring. Yet it also forces pastors to deal with unique situations. Would-be planters, therefore, should count the cost and prepare accordingly.

In this church planting roundtable, six church planters—national and international—explain how they wish they had counted the cost, which yields counsel for the rest of us. We trust their candor will serve other church planters as they begin the work of planting a new congregation.

COUNTING THE COST
Will Forrest

Jesus provides some practical insight on the cost of discipleship: no one builds a house without first counting the cost (Luke 14:25-33). If this is true of building a house, how much truer should it be of the disciple?

There is a cost in following Jesus. So with church planters. We should count the cost of the labor before starting a church. Church planting will cost whatever you are willing to pay. There is no amount of energy, time, relational capacity, or personal health that will not be depleted if you are willing to expend it in your planting efforts.

> "Church planting will cost whatever you are willing to pay."

Within the first few years of our church plant, we watched sixteen new churches around us close their doors. Friends' families endured crises. A lead planter I knew walked away from the faith, and a marriage fell apart. Unfortunately, these stories are not unique to my city. At first watching all this was disorienting, comparable to what a soldier may have felt storming the beaches of Normandy. Once you stepped out of the boat, you were unsure whether the land was any safer than the sea.

My fleshly response was to criticize or question the strategies, intentions, and motives of the guys who had gone before me, which only revealed my ignorance concerning the demands that would soon be placed upon me. The longer I walked the road of planting, the clearer I understood this reality. Church planting will cost whatever you are willing to pay. Therefore, it becomes necessary for the planter to "count the cost," and rightly differentiate between what is being sacrificed to the Lord versus what is being sacrificed to the church plant. Christ deserves our

all. The church deserves our *best*. We can only give the church our *best* when we have reserved the right for Christ to possess our *all*.

DISAGREEMENTS AND DEPARTURES
John Joseph

When I planted Cheverly Baptist Church in 2018, I expected to enjoy a long and fruitful ministry alongside our founding elders. Within three years, however, two of the founding elders left the church over disagreements about the practical application of our ministry philosophy. While I never expected that we would agree on everything, I also never expected that our disagreements would lead to quick departures.

> "We can only give the church our best when we have reserved the right for Christ to possess our *all*."

The effect of the disagreements and their subsequent departure was significant. I questioned whether I was fit to lead. I was plagued by sleepless nights. My wife and I wondered how the church would respond. My kids asked why they left the church. The stress of it all—in combination with several other acute trials—led to me ending up in the hospital. And it wasn't just hard for me. It was hard for those brothers as well. They uprooted their families from a church they loved to be part of planting CBC. Nobody wanted what happened to happen, but it happened, nonetheless. Sometimes brothers see things differently.

Disagreement leading to departures is not uncommon in the world of church planting. Now whenever I speak to prospective church planters, I emphasize the importance of over-communicating with potential elders. Assume nothing. Talk about everything. And when you think you've talked about it all, talk some more. Don't just talk about theology and philosophy of ministry but about pastoral values and the culture you intend to build in the church. At the same time, you can have all the conversations in the world and still have significant disagreements that eventually lead to elders and members leaving the church. If that happens, the good news for you, your family, and for those who leave the church is that God is sovereign and is working all things together for your good and theirs.

UNEXPECTED SEPARATION
Zhang San

I did not expect that church planting would separate "goats" in the congregation. I think that is something every church planter—including those who have a healthy church as their home—needs to anticipate.

As the sending church prepared for the church plant, some church members who lived near the planting destination told us they would not participate in the new plant, even though the new church was a five-minute walk compared to a one-hour subway ride to the home church. "I can't accept a sermon from that pastor," expressed some members. "I just don't want to go," said others.

After a series of difficult conversations, some still decided to stay at the sending church, which is fine, while others changed their minds and decided to join the plant. However, one member was unwilling to change her mind and stopped attending either church. I told her she should feel free to stay at the mother church, but she felt she made herself look bad by being the only person who lived in the new church area but not go to the new church. After reaching out to her for most of the year, she still refused to attend anywhere, and we had to practice church discipline and remove her from membership.

Looking back on this incident, I think we could have done a better job in the following ways:

- Giving the church-planting pastor more opportunities to preach and teach publicly, so that the congregation would become more familiar with him and trust him.
- Encouraging members of the sending church to consider joining the plant as a good thing to do, without making it sound like a necessary or "better Christian" thing to do, so that those who don't want to join the plant for reasons or weakness or anything else won't feel

shamed into doing so or dropping out altogether.

When the whole church is stirred up, false faith will be revealed. Be prepared for this.

INTERNAL CHALLENGES
Joshua Chatman

As pastors, we're to be examples to the flock. This includes modeling a love that "hopes all things" (1 Pet. 5:2–3; 1 Cor. 13:7). Yet I've found it particularly difficult for me to love with a love that "hope all things" after I lay everything out in preaching and then receive little encouragement from the congregation. In those moments, doubts can arise in my heart, like "they don't like me," "they wish I wasn't their pastor," or "they think I wasn't faithful to the text."

To be clear, unfaithful sermons should never be commended. Nonetheless, the absence of encouragement doesn't automatically mean a preacher has been unfaithful or the congregation disapproves of him.

Yet that was my struggle in my first couple of years of ministry. I battled these thoughts and processed them with my wife and biblical counselors. Like a scalpel in the hands of a surgeon, the Lord used their counsel to cut open my heart and expose the cancerous cells of pride that I needed him to remove. My eyes were open to the reality of my problem: fearing man and living for their approval (Prov. 29:25). There's no place for that, especially in

ministry (Gal. 1:10, 1 Thes. 2:4–6). A faithful ministry can't be measured by encouraging responses, because false teachers may be commended while distorting the gospel. Jesus was the most faithful preacher yet severely criticized (Matt. 11:19, 12:24).

I needed the Lord to refine me. I had to mortify my fleshly desires that I might truly love Jesus and rightly serve his flock. In the Lord's kindness, I've grown in this area as the Spirit has enabled me to take thoughts captive, pray fervently, and minister for the pleasure of God and the edification of the saints (2 Cor. 10:5, Mark 14:38, 1 Thes. 2:4).

That's not to say God's ministers don't need encouragement. They do. The Lord uses encouragement to strengthen endurance. Yet pastors shouldn't live for it. In pastoral ministry, commendations from others aren't guaranteed or promised in this age. But if we're faithful to the end, we'll hear the most glorious commendation one can ever receive: "Well done, good and faithful servant" (Matt. 25:21).

LONELINESS AND UNCERTAINTY
Caleb Greggsen

My family and I have faced two specific, surprising challenges in church-planting.

The most consistent challenge is *loneliness*. To be clear, I have another elder for whom I'm deeply grateful and friends in the church. But I left a church with multiple staff members, and now I work alone in my home office. Day-to-day I experience isolation. There are no drop-by conversations with a fellow pastor or even a secretary to talk with in the morning. I must plan every ministry discussion. Few happen organically. In leading a plant outside the United States, there are fewer like-minded churches nearby. I can talk on the phone with like-minded brothers—praise God for that. But that's different from working side by side. I regularly feel lonely in the work. To address it, first, I plan time to fly to the U.S. to be around other pastors whom I know, love, and respect, with whom I can have unfiltered conversations. It takes more effort than driving to a conference up the road, but it needs to be planned.

Challenge number two in planting: the future of a new small church always feels up in the air. Where will the people come from? In the U.S., I often reminded others to be faithful and entrust the results to God. But in the uncertainty of a new, small congregation, empty seats tempt me to anxiety, to worrying about how someone might get angry over a point in the sermon, to losing sleep thinking about what I can do to get the church to grow. Additionally, as a non-citizen, my family's long-term presence feels uncertain. There are questions about our own legal residence that often require hard work and research. Sometimes, I have no answers at all—other than to trust the Lord. I've never been in control of

the future. I'm just much more aware of it these days.

In short, I would tell would-be planters to prepare themselves for loneliness and uncertainty, but then to recognize that this painful, humbling discipline teaches us to work hard and trust God for the sake of the sheep he entrusts to us.

CHURCH PLANTS: VISIBLE SPECIMENS REQUIRING TENDER LOVE
Trell Ross

I think it's *mostly* fitting that we use the phrase "church planting" to refer to starting new churches. I'm not sure why this has come to be the most prominent term, but I would guess it has something to do with the beautiful word picture of a seed growing into something larger and beautiful. Planters hope to see the gospel work of a few people grow into a larger body of Christians devoting themselves to all the God-glorifying work of a church.

As I say, the term fits *mostly*. Where does it fall short?

The term "church planting" can be somewhat misleading. With real plants, seeds lie under the soil for some time before anything emerges above the surface. Not so a church plant. Church plants are visible and require tender love and care from day one. At the outset, there will be culture to build, needs to be met, teaching to be done, people to be cared for, sacrifices to be made by you and your family, and so on.

Why am I telling church planters this? To encourage you to view your church plant not as a plant but as a church from the very first time you take the Supper, if not before. Calculate your expectations both for them and for you. This will serve you and your people well from day one of the above ground living that characterizes a church plant.

W.R. Forrest, Ed.D. Lead Pastor/Planter of Summit Life Church Seattle.

John Joseph is the pastor of Cheverly Baptist Church in Cheverly, Maryland.

Zhang San is a pastor in China.

Joshua Chatman is a pastor of Midtown Baptist Church in Memphis, Tennessee.

Caleb Greggsen pastors an English-speaking church in Central Asia.

Trell Ross is the Lead Planter/Pastor of Pioneer Church in Rock Hill, SC.

The Blessings and Burdens of a Church Planter's Wife

by Gloria Furman

No two church-planting wives are the same. Our unique church contexts, seasons, personalities, challenges, gifts, perspectives, and preferences could fill volumes.

WHAT'S DIFFERENT

If you sat down for chai with Ananya in Ahmedabad and asked her to discuss the blessings and burdens of being a church planter's wife, she may have different things to say than Bonnie in Burnaby, Miriam in Niddrie, or Ana Clara in Sao Paulo. While I'm typing this in Dubai, certain blessings come right to mind—the extraordinary gift of worshiping Jesus with brothers and sisters from more than sixty nationalities and the overwhelming gratitude that members share even in difficult circumstances. Some burdens may include the daily pressure of navigating cultures in such a diverse context and the radiating desert sun that can zap your willpower and the battery in your car.

The loneliness and isolation that one church-planting wife feels may seem like a welcome respite to a wife who compares herself to a goldfish swimming in a fishbowl surrounded by malicious cats. Concerning the spectrum of feelings about support-raising, one month may be like sharing an adventure and the next may introduce a suffocating strain on your marriage.

A wife's confidence in "the plan" to plant a church may waver—even by the hour (and years later). One woman's burden of acute stress in a new context or season may be a blessing in disguise as she learns to depend on the Lord for strength. For others, acute stress may be a red flag to change course.

The unofficial welcome committee may or may not roll out the red carpet for the minister's family. I once heard a story about someone who called the school registrar and impersonated the pastor's wife and took her kids' names off the waitlist for next term. Another church-planting wife says she has a closet full of the gifts that people keep bringing them.

One church-planting wife may already be packing the house when her church-planting husband looks to the horizon and wants to keep planting, and another may feel disappointed.

Persecution may be woven in with spiritual victory over demonic forces; anxiety may stand out on the backdrop of comfort and ease. These and many more contexts, seasons, personalities, challenges, perspectives, and preferences contribute to our uniqueness as church-planting wives.

WHAT'S THE SAME

But some things are the same no matter who you are, what time period you live in, and where God has called your family to plant a church. For one, the conclusion is the same. By faith we all see how our various blessings and burdens are braided together in God's hand as he only gives us everything needful for our good and his glory.

As she surveys the landscape of her blessings and burdens, the conclusion of every church-planting wife is this: *Blessed be the God and Father of our Lord Jesus Christ who has blessed us with every spiritual blessing in the heavenly places in Christ Jesus.* All of the unique factors mentioned above—every single one of them—can and do change. But God and his Word do not change, and the light of this truth illuminates our perspective on all those changeable things.

Church-planting wives need to have the light of God's Word shine on their various blessings and burdens. We need this like we need the sun to rise. We need the light in order to go about doing what we need to do. Two things happen when you turn on the lights in the kitchen. One, you can clearly see what you're doing (and where the coffee pot is). And two, if there happen to be any cockroaches having a slumber party, they'll scatter. When God's Word turns the lights on for us, so to speak, we see reality and the contaminating lies disappear. Blessings and burdens need to be held up to the light of the Word.

APPLICATION

Here are a few floodlights of unchanging truth that every church-planting wife can apply:

1. Jesus, the Chief Shepherd, has been given all authority in heaven and on earth and gives his disciples his mission with his blessing and presence (Matt. 28:18–20). Issues surrounding calling, priority, and fear are all resolved when church-planting wives look to Christ and recall Jesus's utterly comprehensive *authority* to tell us what we're to be about doing, his contagious *zeal* to spread the glory of God among all nations, and his unassailable *power* to provide for us and never leave us as we go about that work.

2. By the grace of Jesus alone can a church-planting wife walk in love together with the under-shepherd whom she married (Eph. 5). As they walk with Christ together, they'll find themselves outside the camp where Christ is, and only with the help of Jesus will they bear the reproach Christ endured. However much they love (or don't love) their city, the husband and wife know their home isn't dependent on his job because they're seeking the city that is

to come. When push comes to shove, as they say, and like Paul the church-planting husband undergoes "the daily pressure on me of my anxiety for all the churches," the church-planting wife takes her cue to boast with her husband of the things that show their weakness and Christ's strength.

3. Jesus loves his Bride, the church, and not even the gates of hell will prevail against her (Matt. 16:18, Eph. 5:25–27). Identity, gifting, and commitment issues are resolved when church-planting wives look to Christ and see how he has made them to be a brick in the building, a sheep in the flock, a priest in the priesthood, and a member of the family. All of these metaphors light up the sparks in her Scripture-soaked imagination as she dreams up ways to build up the body of Christ with the gifts given to her by the ascended Lord Jesus.

Blessings and burdens mingle together as we live in this world that groans for the Day of redemption— now several minutes closer than it was at the start of this article. There's no way a finite heart can hold all the things a church-planting wife will face in life and ministry. But Christ can, he does, and he will.

Gloria Furman is a wife, mother, cross-cultural worker, editor, and writer. She lives in the Middle East, and is a member of Redeemer Church of Dubai where her husband, Dave, serves as the pastor.

Lessons Learned from a Church Planter's Wife

by Jenny Manley

T he Apostles never wrote a list of qualifications for the church planter's wife. That position comes without a title or job description. It comes without compensation. And the hours can be brutal. Also, sacrifices are required, and criticism is likely.

And yet.

You'll get front-row seats to seeing God's work in the lives of his people up close. And you can't put a price on that. Perhaps more importantly, God has much in store to show you personally.

Below are five lessons I have learned in the decade since I first arrived in an unfamiliar city with my husband, who had the task of planting a new church.

1. Life is short; make the sacrifices.

The pressure on a church planter's wife is intense. The job requires a certain scrappiness—making the most of scarce resources, seeing and meeting

> "Should you need reminding, your labors are on behalf of the one institution in the universe that Christ so dearly loves he calls her his bride."

unnoticed needs, and being able to pivot quickly to the next item. It includes encouraging your discouraged husband, tending to needy children, helping a new church member, or showing hospitality to a potential one. Oftentimes you must do all those things simultaneously and usually without much recognition. A church planter's wife can easily drown in the expectations and needs of others. And many do drown in the temptation of self-pity.

After years of tallying the sacrifices I made and dipping my toe in self-pity's alluring waters, I have learned this: life is short; make the sacrifices.

Being a part of the effort to plant a church means you have the opportunity to help build an embassy of the kingdom of God. You have the privilege of working alongside your husband toward something that hopefully will outlast your own life and serve as a demonstration to the universe of the manifold wisdom of God (Eph. 3:10). The church you sacrifice for now seeks to preserve the gospel for the next generation as the "pillar and buttress of the truth" (1 Tim. 3:15). Should you need reminding, your labors are on behalf of the one institution in the universe that Christ so dearly loves he calls her his bride (Eph. 5:22–32).

Our Savior loved his beloved church so greatly that he sacrificed his rights as God, his comfort in heaven, and his very life on earth to create the bride he loves. Keep that in mind, dear church planter's wife, as you sacrifice your husband's presence during another family dinner, a greater than preferred portion of your family budget to meet needs in the church, or the dreams you had for your own life. In the moment, those sacrifices can feel overwhelmingly large. But remember, Christ willingly went to the cross for the joy set before him. Don't fall into a trap of self-pity that keeps your eyes on the here and now. Your life is short and eternity is very long. Make the sacrifices that you have the privilege of getting to make.

2. Church-birth is a season.

I have often thought new churches should be called *church newborns* and not church plants. While the correlations invoked in the agricultural imagery of a church plant are helpful, the process of seeing a new church come to life feels more like bringing a new child into the world. It can be all-consuming; it's often marked by both joy and pain. The effort put into helping a newborn learn to crawl and even walk on her own seems a lot like taking a group of people and turning them into a unified body. Both require sleepless nights, ample nutrition to spur their growth, and lots of encouragement at the slightest cause for celebration. Both are fragile. Both require lots of attention. Both need someone lovingly tending to their needs.

Being married to someone with a church newborn was an intense time for our family. A meeting went well, and we all rejoiced. Conflict erupted among church members, and family plans were scrapped to immediately deal with it. But similar to the foggy newborn stage I experienced after the birth of my own children, that season eventually passed. And in hindsight with both, that newborn season was shorter than it seemed while we were in it.

Dear weary ministry wife, this season will not last forever. Encourage your husband as he invests in good health from the beginning of the life of your church. For all you know, that good health could lead to an early bloom, and your church baby could be walking sooner than you think.

3. Value faithfulness, even over giftedness.

Praise God that he gifts his children with specific ways we can contribute to his church! Over the years of being a part of a church plant, I have seen some people remarkably gifted in teaching, evangelism, and hospitality who have contributed fruitfully to the planting of our church. Our temptation, though, is to place greater value on people with obvious gifts than those whose gifts are not as immediately apparent. Over the years, I have learned that obvious spiritual giftings are not the same thing as faithfulness over time. And long, steady faithfulness produces more fruit than short-lived, zealous giftedness.

> "While the correlations invoked in the agricultural imagery of a church plant are helpful, the process of seeing a new church come to life feels more like bringing a new child into the world."

From my front row seats in the theater of God's work, my eyes may be drawn toward the flashing neon sign on stage. And while I watch what is colorful and bright, I may not even notice the quiet yet indispensable stage crew changing a set. The same is true in a church plant. It is the faithful, sometimes quiet, members who contribute week in and week out to the often unnoticed work of caring for children, praying for those in need, and taking meals to the sick. As the body is built up and learns to care for one another, we create a culture, and we display to the world what it means to be a disciple of Christ (John 13:35). Don't overlook the ordinary faithful members for the fervent ones. Ordinary faithfulness often outlasts zeal.

4. Doctrinal foundations are a necessity.

Do not mistakenly assume theology is only for your husband. Strong doctrinal foundations are the ballast that keeps your ship upright in the storm of church planting. You can get dizzy from the emotional highs and lows of the work, but doctrine stabilizes the ship so you stay the course.

Your ecclesiology will be an aid to the unity of the body, especially as the temptation to grumble threatens disunity. Your steady trust in the authority of Scripture will undergird your confidence that God's Word brings forth life and causes others to flourish under solid preaching. Your love for Christ—both for who he is and what he has done—will spur others on to love him and one another.

Additionally, every ministry wife knows part of her calling is to encourage, build up, and strengthen her husband for the work God has called him to do. When your role is to remind him of truth at the end of a discouraging day, what is it that you say? Do you remind him of God's steadfast love for him? Do you have reason to remind him that the church belongs to the Lord and not to him? Do you speak confidently of the unity God calls us to, which often requires us to keep short accounts toward those who have sinned against us? Take seriously the role God has given you to be a helper to your husband.

5. Trust the Lord, even over your husband.

Ten years ago, when Josh and I got off the plane with our children in our new home, the unknowns of the future far outweighed the comfort of the familiar. Our international move made me feel as if I were stepping off a mountain cliff, and I was uncertain what was going to happen on the way down. As fear wound tightly around me, I remember Josh confidently telling me, "We may or may not plant the church successfully, but what is guaranteed is that we will get more of the Lord."

Over ten years later, I'm thankful we ended up successfully planting the church, but I'm far more grateful for "getting more of the Lord." On the other side of the cliff, the Lord graciously met us and held us tightly. Over the last decade, the Lord has kindly revealed sin, strengthened our marriage, caused us to yearn for his glory, given us a vision for God's heart for the nations, and caused us to see his greatness. John Piper famously said, "God is always doing 10,000 things in your life, and you may be aware of three of them." While the external work God had for us to do over the past decade was to plant a church in the Middle East, I see most clearly what he has done in our hearts to grow us and our love for him.

Jenny Manley is a mother and pastor's wife in the Middle East, where she also spends time writing, podcasting, and serving the persecuted church.

Why Bad Polity Hurt My Church Plant

by Phil Newton

P lanting a church in the 1980s under the aegis of the Church Growth Movement (CGM) involved adherence to its strategists' axioms and principles. Ringing in the planter's ears was Peter Wagner's mantra: "The most effective way to reach people is by planting new churches." The movement's planters followed an agenda for rapid growth and multiplication.

Somewhere in the shuffle of axioms and principles, healthy ecclesiology and biblical church polity got lost. Marketing principles and sociological strategies left the patient work of shepherding a congregation toward spiritual health in the dust. Pragmatism took over.

Sitting under the CGM's gurus convinced me their formula for ministry success was my calling. I implemented several strategies in the church I pastored before launching out to plant in a metropolitan area. But something kept nagging me. *Is this biblical?* For the moment, pragmatism overrode a biblical hermeneutic. I would plant a church and watch it grow.

And it did. But not in a healthy way. I saw the numbers and "decadal growth rate" as foreshadowing my future as a church growth consultant. One problem stood in the way: *the Bible*. Was what I led a biblical church? Were the people joining at a rapid-fire rate biblical Christians? Closer to the heart, was I a biblical shepherd?

> "One problem stood in the way of my growing church plant: the Bible. Was what I led a biblical church? Were the people joining at a rapid-fire rate biblical Christians? Closer to the heart, was I a biblical shepherd?"

My failure at leading the church toward healthy polity can't be blamed on the CGM. I failed to investigate Scripture's framework for governing and leading a healthy church. Pastors are responsible to know the Word. I depended on strategies when I should have slowed down long enough to recognize the obvious. If the church is built on pragmatic methodologies, not on Word and Spirit, then it won't stand when the winds and waves pound away.

PRESUMPTIVE POLITY

While church history shows careful attention by Baptists to church polity,[1] the past few generations of pastors, for the most part, have ignored it. I knew the term and understood it as part of ecclesiology but gave it scant attention. When I planted, I had a presumptive polity. That is, rather than something studied and worked out biblically, I presumed that by meeting on Sundays and Wednesdays, we would just figure out how we were to function together. With the excitement of a new church, it worked temporarily but not for long, and a lack of biblical polity soon exposed weaknesses in our church and my shepherding.

While pastoring in the late 70s before I planted, I witnessed poor polity via unqualified deacons, overly cumbersome committees, power groups, knock-down-drag-out business meetings, and ecclesiological inertia. I overreacted. I presumed that planting a church would free me from these problems. It didn't take me long for the weightiness of ministry and church life to open my eyes to see the desperate need for biblical polity.

LACKING HEALTHY POLITY

If Jonathan Leeman is right that "the trunk and branches of church government [polity] grow out of the seed of the gospel," then the polity-impoverished path I had taken hindered the church's gospel growth and development.[2] Soon, our ecclesial ship— switching metaphors— began taking on water. Five distinct problems arose.

1. Because our church lacked healthy polity, I bore the weight of the church on my shoulders instead of sharing it with the shoulders of a plurality of elders.

Discipling, decisions, counseling, conflicts, worship leadership, details for gatherings, and disciplinary situations—all of it depended on me. The wisdom of plurality in appointing "elders in every city" came to light for me (Titus 1:5).

2. Because our church lacked healthy polity, we had no framework for formally disciplining members.

We had membership, but without a church covenant and stated expectations, we had no recourse when members fell into unrepentant sin. Matthew 18:15–20 seemed like wishful thinking. Sadly, I remember sitting in the living room of a member whom we feared to have fallen into grievous sin with no process to deal with him. It ended terribly. Faithful polity would have addressed this situation for the sake of that man, his family, and the church.

3. Because our church lacked healthy polity, we had no structure for healthy church membership.

The frequent "one another" passages mean little without structure to focus them. It's not that we lacked people joining the church. Instead, we had no structure for examining and holding new members accountable. The front *and* back doors were wide open. Low membership expectations resulted in disunity and carelessness. If good polity grows out of a clear gospel foundation, then it produces the fruit of the flesh, not of the gospel, when it's lacking.

4. Because our church lacked healthy polity, participation in the body was limited.

We made some decisions together. But we needed a congregational structure for meaningful membership, where members engage one another with concern for the church's teaching, direction, and spiritual life.

5. Because our church lacked healthy polity, there was a diminished motivation to raise up new elders.

The pathway to train elders differs from simply mentoring for spiritual growth. Intentionality in training men to shepherd the flock reorients the approach to mentoring. Healthy polity that includes plural elder leadership motivates the pastor to keep training qualified men to serve the flock.

FIVE YEARS LATER

We *sort of* had polity in the church plant. Unfortunately, the polity was between my ears. I attempted to be as biblical as I understood at the time within my cultural and denominational traditions. Even so, nothing was formalized. No documents stated who we were or how we functioned. Nothing spelled out how we led or made decisions. No manual explained qualifications for elders or deacons and how both offices worked out in church life. A *between-the-ears polity* will not work for long.

Around our church's five-year mark, we implemented a well-researched, thoughtful polity. It included a doctrinal statement, a church covenant, membership requirements, a process for church discipline, qualifications and selection process for elders and deacons, and a plan for how officers and the congregation worked together toward church maturity and unity.

But polity on paper, duly approved by the congregation, also meant rolling it out after five years of squishy, between-the-ears polity. We had ups and downs. We struggled out of the gate to get the membership process in place. We staggered through the first group of elders and deacons, trying to learn how to function together. The five-year delay in forming a biblical polity almost wrecked us. But in the Lord's kindness, the body began to see the beauty of biblical polity.

FRUIT OF HEALTHY POLITY

Finally, healthy polity's fruit, worked out of the gospel, began to sprout. Here's what we learned:

1. Polity lays the groundwork for healthy implementation of gospel proclamation.
2. Polity evidences Christ's love for order in his body.
3. Polity frames the divine design for healthy church life.
4. Polity takes the guesswork out of how the church functions.
5. Polity protects the church from the misuse of authority.
6. Polity promotes healthy membership.
7. Polity paves the way for careful shepherding.

The lesson for church planters is labor on developing polity before starting a church. It may need tweaking at points. You may need to clean it up once the dust of planting settles. But if you hold to it carefully as an expression of gospel-centered membership for a local church, it will bear fruit.

---

1. See Mark Dever, ed., Polity.
2. Jonathan Leeman, Don't Fire Your Church Members, 15

Phil A. Newton is director of pastoral care & mentoring for the Pillar Network after serving 44 years as a senior pastor.

Knowing When to Say When: Reflections from a Failed Church Plant

by Derek Bass

W hen I set out with my family to plant a church in Providence, Rhode Island, writing on this topic of church planting failures never once crossed my mind. Instead, we'd envisioned reseeding Rhode Island and southern New England with gospel-driven churches—a line that still rings in my heart from some of our early material—and we'd prayed for our church to be the first of many.

Planting a church in New England, and Providence in particular, wasn't something we did on a whim. I began discussing possibilities with Wes Pastor of The NETS Center for Church Planting & Revitalization while an unmarried doctoral student at Southern Seminary. The conversations continued as I married Elizabeth, continued my studies, and we had our first child. In July 2007, we moved from Louisville, Kentucky to Essex Junction, Vermont to enter into the two-year residency program with NETS, which we extended another two years when I took a staff position at the church.

THE CHURCH PLANTING PROCESS

The process of planting a church from scratch was difficult and slow. We knew it would be tough, but I was perhaps more optimistic than realistic, thinking that planting a church would go a little faster for us.

We began by hosting Bible studies in our home. In the early days, just getting a few people around the living room was a smashing success. Some weeks it was just Elizabeth, myself, and one or two neighbors. After two years of home Bible studies, marriage seminars, and numerous community outreach initiatives (Easter Egg hunts, a movie night in a local park, Bowling Night, a block party) we'd grown from our family of six to around 25 adults and children.

In September of 2013, we began monthly preview services in view of launching in January 2014. The services and the following months were both encouraging and discouraging. A husband and wife that Elizabeth and I had been investing in came to saving faith, but two other couples decided to depart the core team—the former in December and the latter in January. Since adding new people took so long, these kinds of losses felt devastating.

WHEN TO PULL THE PLUG

Answering the question, "How do you know when it's time to pull the plug on the plant?" is to me a bit like shepherding people through suffering. The moment of suffering isn't the time to introduce the reality of God's sovereignty. Rather, we should be *preparing* our people to suffer through consistent and thorough gospel-centered exposition from the whole Bible, building a gospel-centered worldview from which they'll rightly process life in a sin-filled world.

Similarly, church planting is hard work, and you need to set out with a support system. Because, when it gets tough, you need to have brothers and sisters you can be real with. By God's grace, when we set out from Burlington, Vermont to Providence, Rhode Island, we had a strong support system in place: (i) a sending church and its leadership under whose authority we'd placed ourselves, (ii) a mentor who had invested in us for four years, and (iii) a network of church planters I could be honest with and call on in a time of need.

HOW WE KNEW

So how did we know it was time to quit?

First, I'd been struggling with whether pioneer church planting was "my thing" for over a year. In the previous two years I'd received two separate inquiries from schools wanting me to teach in their Old Testament department. One I quickly declined and the other I declined after a brief period of prayerful consideration. But by February 2014, I was beginning to wonder if I'd be more effective for the kingdom by teaching or pastoring an existing church, rather than by planting.

Second, I began to talk honestly with my wife concerning some of my own doubts.

Third, I was in frequent contact with my mentor back in Vermont, my older brother, who was a church planter in the Boston area, as well as a local pastor of another like-minded church (a re-plant) where we'd been worshipping until our church would launch.

As I processed my thinking with these brothers, my wife, and a few others, some things stood out to me:

- The state of churches in Providence in 2014 was much better than in 2007, when we first considered moving and planting a church there.
- We were seeking to plant a church exactly one mile from a very like-minded church, which meant that when people moved to town looking for a church like ours, they'd typically end up there because it was already up and running. This was a big one for me.
- We didn't have any weight-bearing couples in our core team, so Elizabeth and I bore the majority of the weight.
- Whereas a year before, when offered a teaching position, I had no desire, now I felt free and at peace to move on from the plant with no job offer on the horizon. I was experiencing a change of desire.

This final point is clearly subjective, but it's directly related to the first two points; the freedom to move on from the plant was directly related to the changing state of churches in Providence, and in particular my confidence in the leadership of certain churches. Without their faithful and fruitful efforts, I doubt I would have felt such a peace.

Nevertheless, the decision to pull the plug on our plant was extremely difficult, gut-wrenching, and tearful. It left me wrestling through my identity in Christ. It felt like we'd experienced a death in the family.

And yet, as we moved forward, God, our good shepherd, kept his gracious hand upon us, led us into the green pastures of other pastoral ministries, and then opened the door for me to teach in Amsterdam at a missions seminary with over twenty nations represented in our student body. We're now missionaries in secular western Europe, helping to plant a church in Amsterdam and equipping students at Tyndale Theological Seminary on how to preach Christ rightly from the whole Bible by teaching them Hebrew Exegesis and Old Testament Theology. In this work, I regularly draw on my difficulties and past church planting experience as I equip brothers to plant and pastor in some of the most strategic areas of the world.

Our God wastes absolutely nothing.

Derek Bass is an Assistant Professor of Old Testament Language and Literature at Tyndale Theological College in The Netherlands.

Made in the USA
Las Vegas, NV
02 December 2023

81965385R00085